Rod Dedeaux
Master of the Diamond

David Rankin

ISBN: 978-1-60679-251-3
Library of Congress Control Number: 2012955608
Cover design: Cheery Sugabo
Book layout: Roger W. Rybkowski
Front cover photo: Courtesy of the Dedeaux family
Text photos: Courtesy of the Dedeaux family

Coaches Choice
P.O. Box 1828
Monterey, CA 93942
www.coacheschoice.com

Dedication

This book is dedicated to the memory of

Raoul (Rod) Dedeaux

February 17, 1914 – January 5, 2006

Acknowledgments

I am grateful to the Dedeaux family for assistance and advice. Justin and Denise supplied information and photographs and allowed access to documents.

Tom House connected me with the publisher of this book. Special thanks goes to Jerry Merz for his tireless pursuit of phone numbers and addresses of former USC players. Rick Rice sent a mass mailing to the players inviting them to contribute to the book. Their memories of Rod enriched his portrait. I am in debt to all of them.

Stan Charnofsky offered constant encouragement and made useful comments on successive drafts of the text.

Kristi Huelsing and Christopher Stolle of Coaches Choice helped with editing and technical matters.

Foreword

When I was promoted to AAA, everyone was happy for me except Rod Dedeaux. As a Dodger scout, I'd steer him toward the best prospects in high school. Then, he lost his scout. Rod, as usual, was just having a little fun.

He and I did speaking engagements and attended functions together. The fun and laughs could take an entire book. Rod brought warmth and humor wherever he went. Plenty of both are between these covers.

One place we went together was the Los Angeles Coliseum to watch USC football games. For 40 years. Since he died, I've not attended a single game. It just wouldn't be the same.

Rod Dedeaux was more than a great baseball coach. He was a great human being.

He was one of a kind. The world will never see another one like him.

I hope this book will reach a large audience. The achievements of this remarkable man deserve to be known not just by people associated with baseball. His life stands as a good example for everyone.

> Tommy Lasorda
> Baseball Hall of Fame Manager
> Led the Los Angeles Dodgers to World Series titles in 1981 and 1988

Contents

Introduction

I last saw Rod Dedeaux at a USC baseball game. My teammate Stan Charnofsky and I sat in the aisle next to his seat—literally at his feet again. We had played for him in the early 1950s and had recently attended a celebration at Dedeaux Field of his 90th birthday. That day, players from every decade from the 1940s to the 1980s were present. At the game, we had him almost all to ourselves. He was in fine form. He teased and joked and told stories and now and then commented on the action on the field.

Stan and I had heard that he had been approached to write a book. He listed the possibilities—one of which was a coffee table book. We demurred and urged him to write a "real book" about baseball and about life. For him, they were indistinguishable one from the other. We reminded him that he had reams of anecdotes—many hilarious—about events on and off the field. He had a vast storehouse of knowledge about the game and compelling ideas about how it should be played. And he had specific ideas about how it should be taught. All this was contained in a context of rich life experience.

He said he would get around to it. I nagged him by phone and by emails to write the book. He never did. He died at age 91.

A book about him can't be the same as a book by him. It lacks his inimitable voice and material that existed only in his mind. But I went ahead anyway because this remarkable man deserves to be memorialized in print.

This book is not a full-scale biography. It certainly isn't a tell-all book. Even if I knew all, I wouldn't tell it. Warts-and-all biographies and autobiographies are the fashion nowadays and have their place and function. I've chosen to concentrate on the reputation Rod earned for his impact on players, friends, associates, and college and international baseball. Although he owned and operated a successful trucking company, he's known mostly for his accomplishments as coach and mentor. As a man of the world, he's known mostly for his personality—on and off the baseball field. This book, in short, is an attempt to account as nearly as possible for the esteem in which this man of many gifts is held. It is an admiring portrait.

Very little is known about Rod Dedeaux's early years. He was a mesmerizing talker but rarely about himself. He was stingy with personal information, even around his adult children. After he stopped driving, they bought him a tape recorder and urged him to speak into it about his early life while he was being ferried around by a chauffeur. But he needed an audience. Expecting him to speak into a metal object when the live ear of his driver was in the vicinity was like asking Caruso to sing in a closet.

It is possible, however, to locate Rod in times and places during his life. This book begins with a brief biographical sketch that provides a backdrop to what follows. Next is a specific account of the man, his mind, and his methods as the most successful college baseball coach in history. Throughout, the book includes reports from players—famous and less prominent—about how he taught them individually and prepared them to move into professional baseball or into other walks of life. It shows him setting the tone for his program, teaching the game, managing games, and, not least, playing the prankster. It traces his legacy. Finally, an entire section is devoted to testimonials from his players. This book should hold special interest for players, coaches, and fans, but also for the general reader who is curious to know how a legendary man conducted the business of teaching young men about baseball and about life.

Writing the book has put me in touch with teammates and old friends and with players I didn't know personally. Most of all, I again saw Rod in action and heard his voice. He's been called a "role model," a term from pop psychology. The phrase has apparently supplanted that old standby "good example." The exchange is regrettable. "Role" hints of studied artifice. "Model" is associated with transient fashion. "Good example" explicitly names a desirable quality. (Al Capone could have been a role model for thugs aspiring to the top spot.) Rod didn't just leave a good impression. Impressions can mislead or fade. He left a lasting imprint.

1

A Biographical Sketch

Rod Dedeaux once said that in the crib he played not with a rattle but with a baseball. His first steps were probably toward an imaginary base. As soon as he could talk, he might have been chattering instructions to his siblings. The furniture likely wasn't safe when he finally got his hands on an object he could swing.

Admittedly, this scenario may be exaggerated—but probably not by much.

Information about Rod's time in elementary school in New Orleans is skimpy to nonexistent. But working backward from the man to the kid, it's not hard to imagine a bright, energetic boy already becoming excited by the growing power of his talent. A baseball diamond was his natural habitat. He was destined to become a master of it. After his family moved to California, he attended Oakland Tech Middle School. He said kids made fun of his accent. Slim chance that they made fun of his skill on the playground or in the classroom. At age 12 or 13, he was likely the best baseball player in the group. He won all the math prizes. And even as the new boy on the block, he was elected class president. Those kids recognized a leader when they saw one.

After a move to Southern California, Rod earned straight As in the classroom, and as the shortstop at Hollywood High School, he won all-city honors in 1930 and 1931. He won the Babe Ruth Slugging Award and was presented a bat signed by the Babe himself. Once again, as in Oakland, he was elected president of the student body. He was offered scholarships by Yale, Stanford, Cal Tech, the U.S. Naval Academy, and the University of Southern California. He and a couple of buddies from Manchester Playground chose USC because it was the place for baseball. Incidentally, it also afforded him a chance to usher at the 1932 Summer Olympics.

One day, Babe Didrikson, the great female athlete, caught him watching her work out. She said, "Hey, baby face, do you like what you see?" (She was a great athlete but not a great beauty.) She died of colon cancer in 1956 at age 45. By that time, the baby-faced man had established himself as the best coach in college baseball.

Rod's mental acuity for baseball showed early in his time at USC. At a baseball banquet in 2010, the man who was the other half of the double-play combination at USC, Ken Peters, then 94 years old, said he learned more from Rod than from the coaches. In turn, Rod's precocity had been recognized and nurtured by none other than Casey Stengel. Rod and other kids walked all the way from Hollywood to play on the diamonds at Griffith Park. At the time, in the late 1920s, Casey was managing the Toledo Mud Hens and was nearly banned from baseball because of frequent rowdy encounters with umpires. Rod recalled that Casey loved to teach young players and apparently had no trouble making himself understood. (The "Stengelese" came later, as part of his act. Rod once joked that he thought something might be wrong with him because he was the only one in the room who could follow Casey's rambling, ungrammatical monologues.) Griffith Park was known less for baseball than for an observatory, an entertainment venue, and a golf course.

But inconspicuously, except to themselves, Rod and Casey began a lifelong friendship and ultimately had careers that were anything but inconspicuous. As manager of the New York Yankees, Casey won 10 pennants and seven world championships, including five in a row from 1949 to 1953. As coach of the USC Trojans, Rod won 28 conference championships and 11 College World Series titles, including five in a row from 1970 to 1974. No one who might have noticed the baby face and his redheaded tutor could have guessed what was to come. Rod's winning percentage over 45 seasons was .699, the majority of games in what was arguably the most competitive college league in the country: the conference now known as the Pacific-12. His teams had 41 winning seasons. John Wooden, no stranger to national championships in basketball, declared Rod's five consecutive national titles "the greatest achievement in amateur sports history." A mathematician observed that in baseball, the pitcher—the most important man on the field—changes from game to game. The odds of winning five national championships in a row are "incalculable," he said.

By the time Rod played shortstop for USC, he had already absorbed from Casey an education in baseball fundamentals and a reverence for the game. He called Casey "the best baseball mind" he ever knew. He must have learned quickly from his own observations and direct experience on the field. Many years into retirement, he could still remember details of games 30 or 40 years earlier. We can be certain that as a young college player, he missed nothing and used everything.

When Rod played at USC, the baseball facility was a rickety precursor to the current stadium, which was built in 1974 and is named in Rod's honor. The ball team shared a space with the track and football teams. One day, when a track meet and a baseball game were going on at the same time, a javelin penetrated the pant leg of an outfielder and pinned him to the earth. Batted balls rolled into track lanes. Adjacent to the diamond was a wooden structure that served as a music building. (It remained there until the new stadium was built.) A high C was accompanied by the thud of a ball off the boards. In Rod's time, players themselves shaped and groomed what was called Bovard Field. Each step was resisted by other claimants to the territory until the football team finally settled for a practice field behind the right field fence. The track team was moved across the street. The only horticultural remnant was a droopy eucalyptus tree that hung into fair territory along the right field line. It was the cause of more than one controversy.

The layout was quirky. Left field was limited by a street in full use, right field was claimed as a football domain, and center field was a Kansas prairie. The wall and high chicken wire fence in right was so short that pitchers claimed they bumped into it when they went for the resin bag. A couple of them once walked off the distance to demonstrate that it wasn't close to the official 300 feet. That chicken wire was pockmarked with dents from line drives. Football players at spring practice could have used gloves—or their helmets—when a couple of Rod's power-hitting lefties were having a big day. The dugouts were cramped. The stands were comprised of long slats and could hold no more than a thousand spectators. A small concession stand was outside the park near the ticket window. It was in this homely bandbox that Rod won All-Coast honors in 1934 and 1935 as a shortstop, helped the Trojans become a team of note in college baseball, and later put together the best program in the country. He'd be the first to say it wasn't a one-man show by any means, but without him, it probably wouldn't have become a show at all.

On Casey Stengel's recommendation, the Brooklyn Dodgers signed Rod right out of college in 1935 and sent him to their farm team in Dayton, Ohio. Within three or four days of leaving the Delta Chi fraternity on 28th Street, Rod arrived in an industrial town with a population of about 200,000. He had probably taken the train to Chicago and another to Dayton (maybe two trains if he had to transfer in Indianapolis)—a distance of roughly 300 miles. We don't know where he lived: a boarding house, a hotel, an apartment, or with or without roommates. As a big city boy, he must have made some adjustments, as ballplayers always have when packed off to the minors after signing a contract. And as with most of the others, it was probably his first time far away from home and family. A sociable young man excited about his chance to make a dream come true was not, we can be sure, lonely or distracted. But he might have longed for a cool breeze off the Pacific during a hot, muggy summer in Dayton.

The ballclub was called the Dayton Ducks. It was owned and managed by Elbert "Ducky" Holmes, a catcher who had played one season with the St. Louis Cardinals in 1906. He had taken over the team when it became a member of the Mid-Atlantic League in 1932. He was often ejected from games and then went to the stands to continue to heckle the umpires. One time, he harassed them from a perch on a light pole. He kept ducks in a pen beyond the stands. A photo of the 1933 team reveals a duck logo on the shirt. The oddball manager didn't distract the new shortstop. He batted .290 and was called up to the parent team in time to play for the Dodgers on September 28 and 29, with Stengel as manager. The Dodgers were so bad in 1935 that only 184 people were in the stands for Rod's debut as a hitter (he started the second game of a doubleheader on September 29 after being a defensive replacement on September 28). He went 1 for 4, drove in a run, had two putouts and four assists (including a double play), and made one error in a game called a tie after eight innings.

Rod and the Dodgers could not agree on contract terms for the 1936 season. He held out, and ended up playing for the Hazleton Mountaineers, an affiliate of the Philadelphia Phillies. After only 42 games, he suffered a back injury, which prevented him from finishing the season, but it didn't terminate his pro career. He had brief stints of 22 games with the Tacoma Tigers of the Western International League in 1938 and of 30 combined games with the San Diego Padres and Hollywood Stars in 1939. He was probably filling in. He remained active for a few years, playing semipro ball for the Douglas Brothers in Los Angeles.

Many years later, when he was asked about his major league career, he said, "I had a cup of coffee but with no sugar." This flip remark covered a deep disappointment. He became friendly with Phil Alden Robinson, the director of the film *Field of Dreams,* for which he was an advisor. Robinson recalls that Rod said of his missed opportunity, "I think about it every day." (See Robinson's fuller remarks in Chapter 7.) Rod was also an advisor on *A League of Their Own.* He told his daughter Michele that one of the actresses he was going to audition for the movie was named "Mary Magdalene" or something like that. It was Madonna. He said she was a natural athlete, a hard worker, and sweet.

In 1936, with his baseball future in doubt, Rod used his $500 bonus from the Dodgers to buy a truck and go into business with his father. In time, DART (Dedeaux Automotive Repair and Transit) became a major regional trucking firm that made Rod financially independent. The company is now run by Rod's son Terry, who says that as CEO, his dad adhered to the same principles and the same personal approach as those that made him a successful coach. (See Chapter 7 for Terry's full statement.) He never spoke directly to the rumor that he charged USC only $1 a year to coach the baseball team, but he did say that he could have "cashed my check on the Vermont Avenue bus." One time, when he and I were having a beer after practice, he said, "Pick up the tab, Coach. You make more than I do."

During the years when Rod was playing pro ball and establishing his business, Sam Barry was the baseball coach at USC. Sam had been Rod's coach, and between 1930 and 1941, he had a record of 219-89-3 and won five California Intercollegiate Baseball Association championships (before teams began playing in the College World Series). When Sam joined the Navy in 1942, he recommended that Rod take his place in the dugout. That year marks the beginning of one of the most successful coaching careers in American amateur sports. The Trojans finished first in the conference that year and second in 1943, 1944, and 1945 under Rod.

When Sam returned in 1946, he and Rod were named co-coaches at Sam's instigation. Sam joined the team each year after he completed his duties as basketball coach—well into the baseball season. In 1946, 1948, and 1949, the Trojans won the conference title. In 1948, they won the first of 12 national championships. They finished third in 1950, the last year under twin pilots. In the fall, Sam died of a heart attack while he was climbing to the press box to scout California for the USC football team. As Rod said, he "died on duty"—just as he would have had it. Rod's firstborn was named Justin, Sam's real first name, in honor of his coach, co-coach, and friend.

During the years when Sam was in the service, Rod was totally in charge. Although officially Sam and Rod were co-coaches from 1946 to 1950, Rod was the de facto head coach of the USC baseball team. He chose the players, set the lineups, trained the team, and mostly called the plays. He and Sam disagreed on an important call in 1947, and Rod would have been right. Sam said, "After this, you call the plays." This incident is a good example of the mutual respect and affection the men had for each other. More to the point, it showed that Sam was more interested in the team's success than in his own territorial rights.

In 1940, Rod married Helen Jones. Although Helen had also attended USC, they didn't meet until after they both had graduated. Rod suggested Palm Springs for the honeymoon but somehow neglected to mention a ball game that would require his participation. Interests within the marriage didn't always proceed on a one-way street that ended at a ballpark. Helen was already an accomplished artist. One of her designs was in competition to adorn Hancock Hall on campus but was rejected because, as Rod said dryly, it was "too modern." At the time, Helen responded more directly to the criticism that her figures were unrealistic. She promptly painted over the work already done on the mural. ("She had a temper," said daughter Denise.) Apparently, the art critics in the USC administration hadn't caught up with Impressionism. Helen also introduced Rod to ballet, where he was mainly impressed by the athleticism of the male dancers. They were married 66 years, until Rod's death in 2006. They had four children, Justin, Michele, Denise, and Terry, nine grandchildren, and one great-grandchild.

Over the years, I saw Helen (whose nickname was Ditter) a number of times at events and at ball games. Just like her husband, she never forgot a "tiger." She greeted you warmly and asked about your life. Rod's memorial was held on a chilly day at the stadium named for him. Helen was wrapped in blankets. When I paid my respects, she said: "Hi, Dave. I miss him so much." Her eyes were moist and her round face bitten red by the cold. She survived him by only 14 months. Rod set no sartorial example with his taste in flowery sport shirts, but no one ever questioned his taste in a wife. She was a special lady.

Rod cared for his players' welfare as a parent does, but not with a paternal style. He could socialize with them and clown around and invite the team for parties or a meal. (In the early days, Rod said, "Helen would be holding a kid with one arm and stirring a pot of beans with the other.") He did not invite intimacy. He maintained as much distance as he thought necessary to conduct his position. He was always available to players, but not with outward signals of readiness for close personal contact. Individual players might have had reasons for perceiving him as a father figure, or may have had direct experience in which Rod was, indeed, like a father to them. But it was not a persona that he cultivated.

One might easily forget that he was, in fact, a real father with a wife and, in time, four children. Family occupied the top rung in his life, even though it might have appeared from the outside "second only to baseball," as is truly said of some coaches and their sports. Denise said, "We [were] a close family." Starting with breakfast. When the kids were growing up, the entire family took breakfast and dinner together, although it was sometimes late because of Rod's schedule. At that captain's table, just as on the ball field, an upbeat attitude was the order of the day. A pouter would be cause for Rod to invoke the "smile roll call." An artificial gesture, even under orders, can initiate an authentic feeling. It was an antidote to gloom. It was part of a larger view of life that suffused all his activities.

As he said at least once: "I'm a ham." To which his daughter Denise has added: "No doubt, he was a character. He remembered fondly his stint as an extra in movies when he was young." (He claims to have been an extra in *Mutiny on the Bounty,* but she's not been able to find him. She did spot him in the background of a scene in *Death on the Diamond.* She doesn't recommend the movie.)

But life at the Dedeaux residence wasn't all smiles. Rod could summon "the look" and a few words or no words at all—just the look to express displeasure. According to his adult kids, the look was more than enough to discourage misconduct. As on the ball field, he was able to keep the troops in line without trumpeting his authority.

The Dedeaux family wasn't given to taking vacations as such. One time, they went to a dude ranch near Reno and ended up in Susanville, where some of Rod's tigers just happened to be playing summer ball. But the family was scarcely starved for travel. They took trips to Japan for the international series (beginning in 1954), to locations of the Olympics, and even to Italy, where Rod and Bill "Spaceman" Lee gave seminars. In Japan, Rod learned enough of the language to make speeches with the help of a translator, and he taught the entire USA Olympic team a song in Japanese. No wonder his hosts were always pleased when he returned.

One trip does stand out because Rod thought he wouldn't be held to a promise. He doubted that his team in 1971 would win the national championship. "If we do," he told the kids, "I'll take you to the islands." He meant Hawaii. As he emerged from the locker room after the Trojans had, in fact, just won the championship, he was greeted by Michele and Denise doing the hula. Nimble as always, he said, "Catalina is an island." The family went to Hawaii.

At the family's vacation home in Surfside, you wouldn't have caught Rod stretched out on the sand all day to gather that Southern California tan. He didn't need one. His complexion was olive. But you might have seen him bobbing on the water in a huge inner tube from one of his trucks. Or directing a game of volleyball or baseball. Or auditioning and teaching actresses for the movie *A League of Their Own.* Or inside playing host to a variety of guests, including teams from Asia, at one of the many parties at the beach. The family had its own vacation paradise. Or close enough.

Rod was a prominent member of the international baseball community: a tireless ambassador for college baseball, promoter of the College World Series, campaigner for baseball as an Olympic sport, and instigator of an amateur series between Japan and the United States. He received countless awards and honors for all these services, including one from the emperor of Japan. Even his seat at the College World Series was preserved and presented to his family. In 1999, *Baseball America* and *Collegiate Baseball* named him "Coach of the Century."

He moved easily in varied social circles and was a good-natured man with a pocketful of snappy one-liners—many of them original. Beyond the considerable sums he donated, he was available to emcee charitable events. Because he was a raconteur and wit, he was in demand as a speaker.

He was, as the old phrase goes, truly a man of the world.

2

The Man, His Mind, and His Methods

Rod Dedeaux taught his players to believe they could beat any team anywhere at any time—even the New York Yankees. On March 26, 1951, Casey Stengel brought his team to play the Trojans on the USC campus. In that lineup were Joe DiMaggio, Phil Rizzuto, Yogi Berra, Hank Bauer, Jerry Coleman, Johnny Mize, and a rookie named Mickey Mantle. Apart from games at West Point, the Yankees had never before and haven't since visited a college campus to play the home team. When asked how that happened, Rod explained that George Weiss, the Yankees' general manager, and Casey were trying to recruit him either for the front office or as Casey's successor. "They might have been wooing me a little bit," Rod said.

At practice during the week before the game, Rod didn't refer to the mighty Yankees. He concentrated on preparing his team to play a game of baseball, as he always did. Workouts weren't extended. Individuals were tutored as needed. Everyone was expected to carry on as usual. The game wasn't treated as anything special. Nor was the Yankee lineup when Rod went over it before the game. He gave a scouting report on each Yankee in the same methodical tone he used for college players. (Except that he'd take college players with a big reputation down a notch or two. He always granted the edge to his players.) But we all waited to hear what he'd say about DiMaggio. In the same tone, he said: "He has good power to all fields. He likes to pull. Pitch him inside. Don't let him extend his arms." Players exchanged glances. Tom Lovrich, our ace, came too far inside, and Joe lost his hat trying to avoid the pitch. Tom held his breath, but Joe only smiled.

Joe went 0 for 2 that day. But Mickey Mantle went 4 for 5, including two tremendous home runs—one of which Mickey thought was among the longest he ever hit. Rod said: "He's been punishing the ball. Let's start by keeping the ball down." The pitch he hit was about eight inches off the ground, outside, and sinking. He pulled it over the fence in right-center field—on the line and still rising. The Trojans lost 15 to 1. Did Rod expect his club to win? His attitude was that if you're on the field, you expect to win against any and all comers. Otherwise, don't show up. (Years later, he said that USC would still have been in the game if Mantle hadn't scored or driven in nine runs.) Monday, the first thing he said was "You didn't make any mistakes." In effect, you played the game right. That statement summed up his attitude. It was reflected in everything he said and did as a coach.

Setting the Tone

The score didn't work for USC that day, but Rod believed that if you played the game right, the score would take care of itself. He taught the difference between extraneous details and small details that count. Knowing the difference is indispensable to focus. He drilled his teams repeatedly on the fundamentals of technique. He distinguished fundamentals from complicated mechanics. You invest in a play everything necessary to make it—but no more. Even what looked like a casual game of catch was in fact a drill. You aimed at the other man's throwing shoulder and then shifted your feet into a balanced position to return the throw. "Shift those puppies," he'd yell across the field if someone was throwing off balance. He also taught how to transfer the ball quickly but not hurriedly from glove to hand so you maintained a good grip. (Pitchers just playing catch were told to pick a spot and throw to it. In a game, they're required to throw to bases as well as to the plate.) Embedded in "shift those puppies" was his constant imperative: Get into good habits every minute you're on this field.

Bill Faddis, an all-star at a Denver high school and an all-conference shortstop at USC, said he didn't even know how to play catch properly until he arrived at Bovard Field. One day, when Rod was instructing at the batting cage, he noticed that a few pitchers were clowning around during a game of pepper in the outfield. He yelled: "Heads up out there. You're fielding ground balls." (Players used to say that the man had eyes in the back of his head.) Habits, habits, habits. Every situation in practice is a game situation. (More on this later.) Every minute is valuable.

Indeed, good habits are linked. Confidence travels quickly from one location to another. Make a good play in the field because you executed precisely and you'll step buoyantly to the batter's box. Steal a base because you got a good lead and jump as taught and your feet will be nimbler on defense. Even if you're not eventually involved in a play, you should be in a position to execute it properly. Everything is connected—physically and psychologically. Rod taught holistic baseball way before *holistic* became a fashionable term. He might atomize skills when he was teaching individuals, and only later would he demonstrate how they contribute to a larger scheme.

He also taught his teams to act as if they expected to win. But he drew a line between a championship bearing and swagger. His teams were accused of arrogance, but one man's arrogance is another man's confidence depending on whether the viewpoint is inside or outside. If you feel confident, it will show in how you carry yourself. The way Rod's teams carried themselves was intended to intimidate. Lots of coaches set the right tone. They know all about fundamentals. What separates great coaches from the pack is that they're also great teachers.

Work and Play

Rod's system can be explained in detail and thus replicated up to a point. But his methods can't be entirely separated from the man himself. A line from a poem reads: "But how can you tell the dancer from the dance?" He embodied what he taught. To that extent, his success had no secret methods. It was a function of his intelligence and his personality. He was very smart and intuitive, very perceptive, very shrewd, very personable, very articulate, and, not least, very humorous. His presence commanded respect. His players trusted him immediately because they knew he had good reasons for everything he did and said. Grumble they might if they weren't in the lineup, but they never second-guessed him.

One of my teammates said, "You were always a little afraid of Rod." Fred Lynn, who later had a successful career in the American League, said, "Playing for him was a little scary." Not because he attacked players verbally. Not because he ever embarrassed them. Not because he stomped around at practice or fumed on the bench. None of that. His standard call to attention was a plaintive "What in the world, tiger?" But with great respect always comes a little fear. Not fear of what he might do—but fear of what he was. Which translated into fear of disappointing him. Of not meeting his standards on or off the field. He insisted on those standards, drilled them into his players directly and indirectly, and would accept nothing less. In his mind, those standards could and should be met regardless of talent level. They were a congregation of good habits.

Above all, Rod was a great teacher. How did he go about teaching baseball? First, he assumed nothing. "This is a bat and this is a ball." Not in those exact words, but on the first day of practice, Rod started from scratch. He intended to re-educate returning players and to initiate new ones. Stars from previous years and hot prospects were pupils in elementary school. He sent two messages: Everything depends on fundamentals and we are a team.

A grand tour of the bases began in the dugout. "Everyone in this dugout is in the game at all times." You cheer your teammates. You razz the opposition. You yell "back" to a man on first if a pitcher makes a pickoff attempt. You tell your teammates they do or don't have plenty of room to catch a pop-up. You don't challenge an umpire. "That's my job." You look for an opportunity to steal signs. (Unfair? No, it's up to the other team to conceal their signs.) You report to Rod anything—anything—that might be useful. (The pitcher is telegraphing his pitches. The second baseman lifts his left heel when a curve is coming.) If you saw it, chances are that Rod saw it.

He could prowl the dugout, talking to players, but seem to miss nothing on the field. He solicited reports and taught what to look for. Every advantage was valuable. Most of all, minds that were attentive at all times were ready to play if called on. He might suddenly ask a player the count or how many outs in the inning. Not just brains were active on the bench. Rod's teams had a reputation for a rowdy dugout. It was well earned. He cultivated the art of bench-jockeying. No "batter, batter, batter." No profanity. The wittier, the better. A barb can unhinge where name-calling might provoke resolve. Some of the wisecracks emanating from that dugout were funnier than stuff on comedy programs. Santa Clara had a stumpy center fielder named Marcel Fiore. Loud enough for him to hear, Skipper Taft yelled to their first baseman: "Hey, Gussie, throw Marcel a rope. He's going down." (Skipper didn't pitch much, but he did his bit.) A player distracted by yammering would hear: "Hey, rabbit ears, as long as they're over here, why don't you sweep out the dugout." A pitcher losing his poise and his control would be bombarded with a verbal assault and pounding on the dugout. However, if the other team had gone limp, Rod would say "Let sleeping dogs lie."

The Trojans were accused of bad sportsmanship. Rod considered it gamesmanship. Gamesmanship comes in many varieties in sports. It's called "getting into the other guy's head." Rod liked players whose heads were impenetrable, except to what he was saying. Conversely, he liked to probe the penetrability of the other team's heads. Baseball is much more than a test of skill. It's a test of smarts and mental toughness. That test, in Rod's world, was one of the basics.Bench jockeying is now prohibited in college baseball.

The next stop on the tour was the on deck circle, where the team was taught the correct position to coach a runner trying to score and to signal to stay up or to slide to one side or the other. The on deck man also removed the bat to clear the path home. Rod would recall games he'd seen won or lost because the on deck man executed right or fluffed the job. The circle is the perfect vantage point from which to study the pitcher: his motion, the pitch sequence, where he ends the delivery. If he falls off to the left or right, a bunt could be directed in the other direction. The guy resting on one knee was still at work.

At the plate itself, Rod didn't go into detail about batting technique. With one exception: "There's no excuse for not getting the bunt down." He taught the correct stance, how and where to hold the bat, and how to "catch the ball" with the bat, not jab at it. Batters were told to continually notice how the defense was set up. "If the right fielder is playing you way off the line and you hit one down the line, think triple. … If the third baseman is playing you deep, you might want to dump one down." In short, take what they give you. Finally, with feeling: "And for goodness sake, don't look away as soon as you see the sign to take or bunt. We keep some things to ourselves."

Then, a trek up the first base line to the coach's box. Rod placed a lot of responsibility on his base coaches and continually emphasized their importance. They weren't mere traffic cops or appendages. Before the game, they studied the throwing arms and foot speed of opposing players. During the game, they kept a constant eye on defensive arrangements and on the pitcher's move to first. If a runner on first was picked off, he and the coach were fined. If a man was doubled-up on a line drive, he and the coach were fined, especially if neither of them knew how many outs there were—the coach for not warning him in time and getting him back to the base in time. A ragged justice, it might seem, but the point was made.

When Rod got to baserunning, the first thing he said was: "You don't have to be fast to be a good base runner. But you have to be smart." At first base, he demonstrated how to take a lead, how to get a good jump to steal, and how to get back to base on a pickoff attempt. The runner also had to size up the defense to enhance his chances of going from first to third on a single. (Players had already observed the throwing arms of outfielders before the game.) Every effort should be made to take the extra base but not recklessly. "If it's a close play and the guy makes the perfect throw, you did your job. You forced him to make the perfect throw. Odds are that he won't more often than not." Although Rod had a regular first base coach, he expected everyone to pay close attention at this juncture. You might be given the assignment someday.

Second is a hot spot on a baseball diamond. A runner heading to second on what looks like a double play ball is supposed to "take out" the pivot man. Rod emphasized that this tactic is performed with a slide that upends the thrower, not with a tackle or a block. "If you go in standing up, you might be wearing a baseball between the eyes. Infielders have a right to protect themselves." He demonstrated the correct slide—not with spikes up. Once there, a runner has a lot to think about. First, where the shortstop and second baseman are playing in order not to get picked off and to gauge the chances of a ground ball penetrating into the outfield. Then, to remember to take a first step back toward the bag on a line drive so as not get doubled up. Then, to remember not to break for third on a ball hit in front of you. "Be sure—be real sure it goes through."

He'd also say that "third is the easiest base to steal." He'd illustrate how to get a secondary lead and a walking jump toward third. Rod loved this play, and his teams swiped third with discouraging regularity. While at this station, Rod demonstrated how to make the turn at second by hitting the inside of the bag with your left foot, thus avoiding a wide thrust into the outer base path. "The shortest distance between bases is a straight line." This training was linked to his doctrine that "we always take the extra base when we have a good shot."

The tour ended at third base—the last stop before home but not if the third base coach waved the runner to the plate. Once again, Rod's advice was "Send him if you think it'll take a perfect throw to get him." The decision by the coach depended in part on the speed of the base runner. But *all* runners were expected to make turns at bases properly and to proceed from base to base efficiently. Even less than a speedburner might be waved in, especially if the third base coach wasn't impressed by the "hoses" (throwing arms) of the opposition. It was also this coach's job to make sure a runner on second was not picked off. Rod sometimes referred to that coach as "our 10th man."

At third, Rod also covered tagging up on a fly ball and, especially there, not getting doubled up on a line drive. And he explained, for the first time, two situations in which the Trojans play it relatively safe. He never used the suicide squeeze bunt. He expected the batter to get the bunt down and the runner to have gotten a rolling jump—but only after the ball was on the ground. In the same vein, he disliked the contact play, where the runner on third breaks for the plate as soon as the ball is hit toward an infielder, especially the shortstop or third baseman. (The exceptions, of course, are a ball hit to the second or first baseman playing deep or a ball hit hard to the third baseman with one out and another runner on first. You force a throw to the plate and avoid the double play.) He abhorred running into outs. To the man on third: "Make the ball go through. If it does, you can walk home."

That ended the tour. He expected players to grasp everything they heard on the tour. Not yet into their bones, perhaps, but certainly in the front of their minds. And they would remember how many times during the tour he stressed cooperation and used the word "smart." Omitted from this sketch are anecdotes—some funny—that he drew from his astonishing memory to help players visualize the lessons. Those lessons would be reinforced at practice and during games—sometimes for the entire team and sometimes for individuals. The biggest aid to memory was Rod's ability to encapsulate a point in a few words. And as in everything else he did, he was convincing his players that when they took the field, they would "play the game right."

The tour laid the groundwork for Rod's instructional program. It defined "the Trojan way": Baseball is essentially a mental game. For newcomers, it was the first example of the master at work. All that was dispensed on the tour might seem elementary. That was the point. Anyone who watches baseball can't fail to notice how often the relay play is botched by professionals. An outfielder will throw to the feet or side of the relay man—possibly because the relay man isn't waving his hands above his head as a target. Or the outfielder will miss the relay man altogether. In turn, relay throws are often off-line—up one baseline or the other. Or they're thrown all the way in the air instead of on one bounce, leaving the upright catcher at the mercy of an incoming runner. Relay throws that miss the cutoff man allow runners to take an extra base. ("Don't give 'em a free base. Make 'em bunt and give up an out.") As Rod taught repeatedly, the relay man should be stationed on a direct line between the outfielder and the plate and the cutoff man should also be in that direct line. "The shortest distance between two points." Efficiency again. Always efficiency. The correct way to execute this play was rehearsed over and over in practice until it became second nature. "If you have to think, it's too late." A good throw should be automatic. Accuracy. Accuracy. "Bad throws are mental mistakes."

Inferential genius wasn't required to grasp the general point: Be in the right place at the right time and execute perfectly. Set up what you intend to accomplish. All hands know their function and are coordinated to achieve a goal. Not just on a ball field. That commandment applied tartly to infielders. Rod was more forgiving of booted balls than of errant throws. Infielders were taught how to play hops, how to set their feet and bodies, and how to release the ball from the most propulsive angle until these movements also became second nature. But he didn't hold out for balletic fluency. Of a play that wasn't picture perfect, he'd say, "Not the prettiest way, but it was one way."

Training of infielders as individuals was the foundation for teaching how to execute the double play. One day after practice, when I'd finished running my sprints, I watched Rod instruct our sophomore second baseman and shortstop in the art of turning two. He was still nimble at 39 and with a balky back. First, he played the pivot man at second and then at shortstop and directed the feeder to make bad throws. He caught every one but didn't always relay the ball to first base. He kept saying, "You cannot drop the ball no matter how bad the throw is." Then, he taught the players how to position themselves for the double play, how to cheat a few steps toward the base depending on whether the batter was a righty or a lefty, how to get to the base the quickest way, how to make and take the feed, how to use their feet, and how to throw to first. He pared away all extraneous movements. It was as though he had counted the necessary movements and steps in the most direct routes. Maybe he had.

Then, came the capper. "I was teaching you how to handle bad throws. But there won't be any bad feeds from either of you. It will go to your partner's throwing shoulder. You cannot make a bad throw. It's a mental mistake." Then, he grabbed a fungo bat and hit ground balls to make the two young infielders practice what he had just illustrated. All the while, he kept repeating the key instructional phrases so they entered an echo chamber in the brain. If he had said "Make sure of one" or "Don't drop the ball," the essential point would have been made. But as was so often the case, the choice of words and the music added resonance to the point: "You *cannot* drop the ball." What's more likely to stick: "Be sure of one" or "You *cannot* drop the ball"? The voice gave not a command but a commandment. It might have been inscribed on a stone tablet.

Rod had an extensive repertoire of words and music. Where risk was involved, he'd say: "Be sure. Be real sure. "The words were drawn out—the vowels in "real" elongated. It applied to trying to steal a base on your own. For pitchers, it applied to trying to induce a foul ball for strike two, especially on a count of no balls and one strike. The chummy right field fence at Bovard was an inviting target for lefties with power. They were accustomed to seeing pitches low and away—sinkers or fading change-ups. When they saw what looked like a juicy pitch, their eyes lit up and their bats twitched. The pitch that Rod taught was directed at or above the letters and a good four or five inches inside. You had to be "real sure" that the pitch didn't drift over the inner third of the plate. Properly delivered, especially after a called strike one, it usually resulted in a hooked foul ball. Those fouls could be long and loud but officially were nothing more than a strike on the record.

In contrast, Rod never said "Be real sure" when it came to taking an extra base or scoring from second on a single. You went if you thought it would take a perfect throw to retire you. Judgment was called for. You were expected to know the throwing arms of the opposition and where the defense was stationed. You were expected to get a good start on the play if the ball was definitely a hit. It was a gambler's play, but you had to hold good cards. You didn't force the odds. You rode them.

When Rod said "Bull your neck, tiger," the tone was crisp but not corrective. He wasn't suggesting that you hadn't been doing your best. It was a call for resources he knew you had. It was a direct appeal to the gut. At times, he might have said "Hang in there" or "Bear down," but the imagery in "Bull your neck" in itself evokes a grittiness that the blander expressions lack. (Tommy Lasorda gave Orel Hershiser the nickname "Bulldog.") We also understood that bulling the neck didn't mean "forget what's above it." It was a call for full power of concentration. Make the next pitch even better than the last one. He was giving a booster shot, not a recovery shot.

Each of Rod's pithy directives had its own music. "You cannot drop the ball" sounded ominous. "Be real sure" had an echoic effect. "Bull your neck" was a pointed summons to action. His all-purpose injunction was "Show me something." It had the ring of someone waiting and expecting to be impressed. The "me" really *meant* him. It wasn't a vague pronoun, as in "We'll see you later." Accompanied by a couple of claps of the hands and a cock of the head, the tone was chipper and upbeat. He was the methodical coach as cheerleader—for a minute.

To a pitcher arriving from the bullpen, he'd say, "Hold 'em right there." If USC trailed, he'd add, "And we'll win this one for you." Rod's voice, as he handed the pitcher the ball, communicated a transfer of responsibility from coach to player. In effect: "I've made the move. Now it's up to you." He might add a few words if the catcher and infielders were clustered around the mound. "Watch for the bunt." "Let's get two." But the meeting wasn't social hour. Nor was he calling for something he didn't expect. When he turned his back and jogged back to the dugout, the steps were stiff legged and tidy, with his hands loose at his sides. He didn't stride to or from the mound, as if to present an image of determination and authority. I don't recall his patting the pitcher on the back or on the rear end, as one sees major league managers and pitching coaches do regularly. He'd just shown his trust in the pitcher. He completed a necessary transaction without fanfare—as usual. Anyone watching closely would get the impression he'd just made a course correction in keeping with a master plan. Above all, the pitcher was supposed to get that point. Demeanor influences demeanor.

Rod's words, music, and body language were noteworthy not just in themselves but because they were adapted to specific individuals and situations. He had a "feel." At times, he'd say "You pick your spots." This applied equally to leaving things alone as to taking action and to making it count when you take action. Too much "over the top" dilutes the impact of over the top. And it wastes energy—moral and mental. It sets a bad example. Simplicity doesn't mean simple minded and certainly not simplistic. It means "only as much as needed with no superfluity." As such, it's the basis of elegance. Rod's simplicity was elegant.

Demeanor can be broken down into its components, but it can never be fully accounted for. It can be faked up to a point. Even then, it will seem out of character for a person you know well. It has its uses. Behavior that has shock value isn't without momentary effect, but it can backfire. Rod was aware of this possibility. He normally stuck with who he was. He was a man of many parts—each genuine in the moment if genuine is taken to mean lodged in the core person. In the end, all one can say is that Rod's demeanor was a function of the whole person. It was there to observe but not to explain.

During batting practice, Rod would sometimes amble on the lip of the outfield grass and continue to instruct infielders as they took ground balls live off bats. "Stay down. Soft hands. Shift your feet. Throw right." One might fret that he'd ruin concentration by inserting himself into the trenches under fire and chattering at the troops. (He'd be the first one to yell "Look out" if a line drive was headed at him.) But he expected those directions to already be in the players' heads. He provided the live echo. And he also expected the players to distinguish between distractions, which they ignored, and reinforcement, which they continued to internalize. In teaching, he believed you could never have too much of a good thing. Above all, you concentrate no matter what's happening around you.

Pitchers were taught that they were the fifth infielder. Pepper games were intended to sharpen reflexes to field balls hit back to the mound. On the bunt play, you were determined to retire the advanced runner. Pitchers were drilled over and over on how to field a bunt and throw to the advanced base. With a runner on second, the batter's job is to get the bunt past the pitcher to make the third baseman field it. In that situation, USC pitchers were trained to break toward the third base line as soon as they released the ball in order to intercept the bunt and then get the runner at third. The runner was to be pinned down with a short lead. "If they want to bunt, make a pitch to bunt. We want the out at third." With no outs, the other team might try to move the runners up so the man on third could score on a sacrifice fly. But that team wouldn't try to sacrifice again with one out. Nothing is gained by having a man on third with two outs. Rod baited the other team into sacrificing the advanced runner, not the man laying down the bunt. But if the runner on first has been disallowed a big lead and the pitcher is *thinking* "Get the guy at second," he'll be ready to bounce off the mound and pounce on the ball. Once again, anticipating success is a spur to action. You can't make a play without imagining you can make it. Then, you have to believe that you can make it. In these bunt situations, Rod would say "While we're at it, let's get two"—the runner *and* the bunter. What he meant was that the pitcher and the entire infield should have their minds set on a double play.

Roy Smalley, who had a long major league career and was an all-star, recalled that during the week before the College World Series in 1972, Rod drilled the team relentlessly on how to retire the advanced runner at third on the bunt play. The players grew sick of the endless rehearsal. Cut to the championship game against Arizona State.

In that game, the Trojan pitcher fielded a bunt with no outs and threw the advancing runner out at third. On the next play, the USC infield turned a groundball into a double play. USC won the game 1 to 0—and earned another national championship.

Rod left mechanics to pitching coaches. If he saw something he didn't like during a game, he'd mention it. His work with pitchers was directed mostly to state of mind, beginning with: "Remember, nothing can happen until you decide to release the ball. You're in charge. You set the pace. You establish the rhythm."

Tom Seaver, a Hall of Fame pitcher, said: "I didn't learn to throw a slider from [Rod], but he taught me more important things. I learned about passion for the game, about concentration, about being part of a team. He taught us how to conduct ourselves in a uniform." No pitcher learned to throw any pitch from Rod. But he oversaw the old-school line in conditioning. His regime was simple: lots of running and stretching and hanging from a bar. Before the era of pitch counts, the pitchers who started games on weekends and were expected to finish them might also work an inning or two in nonleague games during the week. Sore arms and injuries were rare.

High on Rod's list of assets for pitchers was fortitude. He knew that fortitude can't be taught or instilled. It's probably a function of temperament and early life experience. He was a practical psychologist but not a psychotherapist. But he also knew that concentration can help cure the yips if they're curable. A person totally immersed in his job is less likely than otherwise to suffer the jitters. On the matter of courage, or "guts," he took people pretty much as he found them, made his assessment, and tried to match the man and the situation. Pitchers who "wanted the ball" and prospered under pressure were his kind of guys. And he let them know it. They were the first to get the ball and the last to be relieved of it in stormy weather. He'd come to mound and say: "You're fine. Bull your neck, tiger. We'll get out of this." Like everything else he said, you believed it—in large part because you believed that he believed it.

As the saying goes, the risk of leaving the pitcher in "one batter too long" is always present. Unless a pitcher was getting shelled or walking batters, Rod seemed ready to take that risk in order to allow a pitcher to finish an inning and vacate the mound voluntarily. (Of course, the score, the inning, the opponent, and the venue were considerations.) The pitcher might not return to the mound the next inning if Rod thought his day was over, but the young man had finished the day more or less on his own terms. Rod took risks to build confidence. You knew he'd always try to avoid making you look bad. The reverse was his preferred method.

Sometimes, when I worked with the pitchers, Rod would come to the end of the dugout and signal that the pitcher warming up should get to within five or six pitches of being ready to go. (That is, warm-up pitches on the mound.) He might not have been quick with the hook, but when he used it, he expected the next man to be mentally and physically prepared to take over. The coach in the bullpen had to insist that the man warming up throw strikes—preferably low ones. Walks by relief pitchers aroused in Rod visions of a reserved seat in hell for the man. In this world, the cost was a fine. The pitching coach might also hear a few words.

All training on defense was predicated on thinking ahead. You anticipated what might happen and thus were ready to make a play or to position yourself as a participant. The right fielder came forward in case of an overthrow at first. The center fielder came forward to back up at second as soon as a steal was in progress. The left fielder came forward on an attempted steal of third. In repeated drills, pitchers were taught to cover first on a ground ball to the right side. And as a reminder that they weren't invincible, they were trained to back up third and home on hits against them with runners on.

Rod was a bear about defense. It paid off. Time and again, the right play, not necessarily a spectacular play, made the difference in a game. Stan Charnofsky, our second baseman, was held after practice one day to field a long series of ground balls hit to his left on their way into right field. They were hit increasingly harder and deeper. He scampered laterally into the outfield to catch them, learning to gauge the best angle on the ball. "It's still a short throw from there, tiger." Stan came to the locker room with his tongue hanging out and mumbling words well short of adoration for Rod. The next day, Stan made that play look routine for the last out when the other team had the tying run on third.

Rod preached that a ruthless defense puts pressure on the opposition and can take the heart out of them. Its biggest value, perhaps, is that it keeps things from unraveling into the big inning. In addition, even when a relay doesn't get the runner or a double play misses by a step, the other team gains no comfort by noticing that the plays were made perfectly. The opposition might not try to take the extra base next time. A play made right is a cautionary tale in itself. ("We look good at all times, tigers.") In that game against the Yankees, the defense made no mistakes—except to play Mickey Mantle inside the ballpark.

As a batting instructor, Rod didn't tinker much with mechanics. He might correct a long uppercut swing or an off-balance stride or a head pulling off the ball. But he was leery of making too many changes even to a young player's batting style. It was largely determined by anatomy. Hand-eye coordination, strength, and wrist action all came in the basic package. Rod worked mostly with what came naturally. He didn't clutter a batter's mind with minutiae about the deployment of feet, fingers, hands, shoulders, and head. Typically, he concentrated on the mental approach to hitting. He had a key phrase: "your pitch." Whenever you saw it. It could come on the first pitch or deep in the count—right up to two strikes. The pitcher is trying to make you hit "his pitch" (or swing and miss) and you're trying to get one you like. Every play in baseball begins with this contest. (Baseball is the only sport in which the defense goes first—unless you count the kickoff in football.) In Rod's world, you didn't go to the plate to see what the pitcher has or to run up his pitch count. You went to hit him or to draw a walk—preferably the former. (Pitchers may get upset with themselves when they walk batters, but their confidence is rattled when they give up hits.) The sooner, the better. But "make it your pitch."

Rod would stand by the batting cage and say things like: "You have to lay off that high pitch. You'll pop it up." Or: "Don't try to pull everything. Take the outside pitch the other way." Or: "There are two strikes. Choke up on the bat a little." Or: "The count is three and one. Visualize the pitch you want. Look for it. Take if you don't get it." Or: "There's a runner on third with less than two outs. You have to put the ball in play." Or: "The hit and run is on. You can't miss the pitch. Hit it the other way." The batter was literally surrounded on three sides by a cage. But he was prompted to imagine that he was in a game. Rod's drills simulated real games.

Interestingly, Rod didn't insist that "your pitch" always had to be a strike. He knew that bad ball hitters, like Yogi Berra, could whack what they saw coming even if it was at the eyes. Rod wouldn't recommend that to his youngsters, but he allowed leeway to batters who could get around on a fastball four inches inside without pulling it foul or could go with a pitch four inches outside and drill it into the right field corner. Ed Simpson could put a strong inside out swing on an a fastball that nearly grazed his belt buckle and drive it into right-center field. He led the nation in batting average.

Rod also realized, of course, that you'd have at bats when you didn't see anything close to what you liked. You tipped your hat to the pitcher. You did the best you could with what you got. But the principle of "your pitch" still obtained. So did "Jump on it as soon as you see it." I think Rod would call this approach "smart hitting" rather than the more voguish "aggressive hitting." I never heard him use the term "aggressive." To his mind, it smacked a little of "out of control"—the last thing he wanted to see in a Trojan ballplayer.

A running team is a sliding team. Rod was an exponent of the hook slide or the fadeaway slide. Players—and pitchers too—continually practiced this slide in a sawdust pit until they had wood chips up to the gills. True to form, Rod could make the exercise seem like a kids' game and deadly serious at the same time. A tumble after a botched effort might evoke "When do the seals come on?" Or worse. He forbade the headfirst slide. "If you ever see a sprinter slide across the finish line, you can do it. Stay on your feet. You'll get there faster."

In summary, Rod taught his teams to force the action on offense and to smother the action on defense. Put that way, the program sounds simple. And it was simple—even elegant—as are all core ideas. (Einstein said, "Everything should be done as simply as possible but no more simply.") Rod had no junk in his mind. His ideas had a geometric clarity that insisted on precision, rigor, and concentration—all three necessary to success on and off the ball field. Players knew he was teaching more than baseball. Even an 18-year-old can fathom that ideas are transferable from one domain in life to another. Perhaps the point wasn't grasped right away—perhaps not analytically—but it was directed at a deeper level: in the fiber, where substance, once lodged, becomes entrenched.

Simple ideas require a special kind of work because they must achieve an intensity of focus that eliminates distractions and frills. They demand a commitment to execution that makes cohesive what otherwise might seem a collection of bits and pieces. In baseball anyway, the center can hold if all action—mental and physical—is brought to bear on it. Energy that skitters to the margins is wasted. It may seem that Rod is being presented as a taskmaster. He was. Bill Lee says in his book *The Wrong Stuff* that Rod "ran a tight ship." He did. But not like a drill instructor or like Woody Hayes. He can be called a disciplinarian only if that term is stripped of its harsh overtones. Roy Smalley said: "Rod's genius was for getting everybody to buy into his thinking of how to play the game and how to behave. One amazing thing was his ability to be a disciplinarian without you knowing he was."

To start with, Rod was a gentle and sensitive man. He understood people as well as anyone is capable of understanding someone else. At times, he seemed almost able to read minds. When he talked or listened, he was fully engaged. Like all great communicators, he had a refined sense of audience. He knew the ins and outs of every player. You could see it in his eyes and hear it in his tone when you were the audience. The message was tailored to you. It was designed to make his players feel important. Not just on the ball field but in and of themselves. It was, perhaps, his greatest gift—one that he cultivated into a fine art. A Frenchman once said "Style is the man." If he had observed Rod at work or socially, he'd have said "See what I mean."

Rod's most intimate method of individual attention was known as "a shave and a haircut." A player would find himself being escorted up the first base line (usually) by a man massaging his shoulder and talking softly into his ear. A tiger was "getting the works." It was assumed but never made explicit that the conversation was private. It might cover technical information but most often was Rod's response to a perceived issue with attitude or behavior. The issue need not be blatant, which might call for an office visit, but rather something that Rod wanted to straighten out pronto. No matter what was said, the end product was encouragement. Without going into specifics, players would say: "I thought he was going to lower the boom. I'm not even sure what all he said. But I don't think he can do without me." Or words to that effect.

During these ambles, Rod did most of the talking. Some of it was an attempt to draw a player out—to discover what was on his mind, especially a troubled mind. What troubled a player troubled Rod. He was particularly deft at clearing up misconceptions and was prepared to grant they might exist on both sides. A tone of sympathy was maintained, even when the content wasn't entirely sympathetic. Few—if any—players emerged from that tête-à-tête without a mutual understanding. Rod expected it to stick. He'd repeat technical or strategic instruction over and over, but a personal message was meant to hit home the first time. And stay there.

Although Rod was a low-key critic, his expectations were ubiquitous. They were in the air if not on his tongue. Pressure came with the territory at Bovard Field and Dedeaux Field. He said: "When we work, we work hard. But we also have fun." Some of it came from jokes players pulled on one another. Some of it was standard locker room banter. But most of it originated with Rod himself. He was the prankster in residence.

He possessed a red wig made from real hair. He could part it down the middle, comb it over the ears, or fluff it up wildly. The thing looked uncannily real no matter how he arranged it. On the inspiration of the moment, he'd fashion it either to contradict or to exaggerate his victim's natural look. You knew he'd pop it on you somewhere in some outrageous form on a road trip—usually your first as a member of the varsity. But you didn't see it coming. Suddenly, a player about to enter a high-class restaurant in San Francisco would be diverted into a restroom and fitted with the wig. No looking in the mirror. Then, he'd be escorted slowly and deliberately to a table, where his teammates would give no hint they had been joined by an incongruous intruder.

Before long, first the waiter and then customers nearby would be trying to conceal, unsuccessfully, their disbelief that a USC ballplayer was allowed to wear crazy hair—red at that—among his well-groomed buddies. People whispered to or nudged a table partner, who would then try to sneak a look. The bewigged one wasn't permitted to foil the prank either by speech or demeanor. Above all, no flamboyance that would give the game away. Nor was he allowed to sit silently. The rule was "act natural." The rule for someone in those circumstances should have read "Act as if you're acting natural." Perhaps now and then a frustrated actor enjoyed the show he was starring in. But players less flattered by conspicuous attention did their time, so to speak, more or less stoically and, finally, in the spirit of fun. The ceremony was, after all, an initiation. You had made the Trojan traveling team.

When I got the wig, Rod narrowed the range of the audience. He invited me to join him in the lounge car on a train ride from San Francisco to Los Angeles. He stopped me in the passageway, plopped on the wig, tried a few arrangements, his eyes as intense as those of a Beverly Hills stylist, until I could feel on my forehead the tickle of bangs that added no sophistication to *my* baby face. In blazer, white shirt, and repp tie, I might easily have been mistaken for a preppie being hauled home by Daddy after expulsion for violating the hair code. (This was 1951, not 1971.) "There, that should do it," he said. It certainly did. He led me to a chair across from a pretty woman, probably in her 30s, expensively dressed, her legs discreetly crossed. She was reading a magazine. She looked up to smile at us, held the smile, frozen, for a few seconds, then abruptly lowered her head to the magazine. But not for good. She checked a few times to make sure the mismatch of wardrobe and hair wasn't an apparition. Someone later heard a good story.

Back in the passageway, Rod said: "I think she's interested. She couldn't take her eyes off you." I'll bet. Between the shave and haircut and the red wig, Rod kept busy at his two versions of the barbering trade—one earnest to a fault and the other ridiculous to a fault.

Then, we had the case of the shrinking finger. An assistant coach named Serge Freeman wasn't fond of any airplane he happened to inhabit, especially in the dark. "Those night flights are bad," he'd say. The morning after one of them, while Serge was showering in their Portland hotel room, Rod switched the rings they had earned as members of the 1948 National Championship team. Somehow, he had ended up with Sam Barry's ring, on which the initial B had become smudged. So had the initial F on Serge's ring. The second initial on both rings was unclear. This fortuitous circumstance was too good for Rod to resist. He also knew that Sam's ring was wider than Serge's. How he knew such things is a measure of his penchant for espionage—on and off the ball field.

Rod watched as Serge toweled off, got dressed, and slipped the ring on his finger, catching it just in time as it slid down to the knuckle. He tried again to keep it in place. Same result. While his roomie was examining the ring, Rod said, in his most solicitous tone, "What's the trouble, coach?" Serge rather sheepishly described the weird event. They agreed that the ring couldn't be at fault. It was on the dresser exactly where Serge had put it before he showered. The initials looked the same as always—the S clear and the F (so Serge thought) blurry. The inescapable conclusion was that Serge's finger had shrunk. "I told you those night flights are bad," he said. Rod said: "The atmosphere up here is damp. Maybe your metabolism has been affected. You probably need a good sweat." Not that either of them knew how metabolism might somehow be involved.

They decided that Serge would pitch a long stint of batting practice before the game that day. After the game, again while Serge was in the shower, Rod switched rings back. (Rings were kept in a valuables bag. Rod got there first and recovered Sam's.) With a broad smile of relief, Serge held out his finger, on which his actual ring fit snugly. "Look," he said, "it worked." Rod said: "Good. No more blaming night flights."

Next morning in the hotel room, Rod again pulled the switcheroo. Serge, struggling to make the ring fit, was even more perplexed than on the first occasion. Maybe he should see a doctor. A shrinking finger is nothing to take lightly. It had never happened before. His entire system might be out of sync. But Rod persuaded him to take one more long tour on the mound. "If the ring doesn't fit after that, we'll get you to a doctor in a hurry." The "remedy," of course, worked a second time. The finger was fully proportioned, but Serge's arm must have been dangling at his ankle. On a day flight home on Sunday, according to Rod, Serge kept checking to make sure that ring and finger were in harmony. In the next seat, Rod inquired about the finger, apparently seeking reassurance. He said, "The workouts did the trick."

It's not recorded that Serge ever again visited the Northwest. But he was a presence on Bovard Field as a player and as an assistant coach. The story about the shrinking finger has a certain symmetry because Serge himself was a funny man in a funny man's sport. A lot of baseball humor is very broad. Serge was droll. You had to pay attention and listen closely or you might miss his best lines. I always contrived to sit near him on the bus. He never swore or used sexual innuendos. But he wasn't averse to taking nips out of players, including our own. (I remember some of these cracks, but they're better left unrecorded.) He kept us loose in the bullpen.

After leaving USC, Serge coached at Inglewood High School and El Camino College, where, to my knowledge, he was the first coach in Southern California to abandon the old heavy flannel uniforms in favor of the lighter cloth that later became standard in the sport at all levels. He designed a scorebook and published a book entitled *Basic Baseball Strategy* in 1961, which major leaguers could benefit from reading, lest they neglect the fundamentals. In spring training in 2012, Kevin Youkilis, then with the Boston Red Sox, said, "We're going over things that we've probably forgotten." Serge's book is rich in reminders.

Billy Wills was another Trojan not on friendly terms with airplanes. In fact, he was about to board one for the first time. As the team began to file through the gate toward the aircraft, the PA system blared "Telephone call for Mr. William Wills." Rod said: "You better get it. It might be important."

Everyone was seated on the chartered DC-3 when Billy came running across the tarmac. The stewardess greeted him at the door and said "Where have you been?" He said: "I had a phone call. But no one was on the line." (Guess who made the call.) He started to mount the steps. The woman said, "Where's your parachute?" He was taken aback. "What parachute? Nobody gave me a parachute." She said: "Well, it's too late now. Get in." He backed onto the tarmac. "I'm not goin' without a parachute." Their debate was in full progress when the captain stuck his head through the door. "Son," he said, "you're holding up this flight. I have instructions to take off."

Billy boarded, with his face pale and his eyes googley. A seat next to a window had been reserved for him. No one said a word. He didn't observe that no parachutes were in sight or maybe he thought they were under seats. As the plane gathered speed along the runway, Billy stared into the seat ahead and grasped the arm rests with taut fingers. Even after he was told 15 minutes into the flight that others were also without parachutes, he wasn't reassured. "I hate airplanes. They should have parachutes." The captain came into the cabin, leaned over to Billy, and said: "Relax. I've flown this route a thousand times. You'll be on the ground before you know it." Not soon enough for Billy. He remained as rigid as a doorstop until the wheels hit the ground in San Francisco. In games that weekend, Billy, always a ferocious hitter, pummeled the ball. Solid earth was his milieu. On future trips to the Bay Area, he drove his own car a day ahead of the team and drove home on Sunday. On longer trips, he endured time in the air but never with any noticeable adjustment to the confines of "the big iron bird." This kind of practical joke may be thought cruel or at least "insensitive" nowadays, but no real harm was done. Billy himself could laugh about it—as long as he was on the ground.

In sillier moods, Rod might don those black frames with bushy eyebrows and a big nose and ham it up. On a rare occasion when he was ejected from a game, he left the field, returned wearing the wig and sunglasses, and sat in the stands. The umpire couldn't figure why people were laughing when nothing funny was going on. Rod also had so mastered double talk that a listener might think his ears were failing. Rod's voice would rise and fall as if it had real content—sometimes to indicate a question. The listener knew that an answer was expected, but he had no idea what he'd been asked. Rod would then put on a quizzical look, as if the to say "Well, I'm waiting." But before he departed, he made sure that auditors didn't feel offended. A couple of players about to board the team bus asked a hotel doorman what Rod had said to him. The man said: "I'm not sure. But he's a great guy." Charm doesn't rely on making sense.

Many jokers can dish it out but not take it. Not so Rod. Players could tease him about his shirts or his pink Cadillac with big fins. Jack Schlarb, a fireballer with a clownish aptitude himself, once entered the locker room, cast an eye on DEDEAUX on Rod's traveling bag, and said, "Who is this guy DAYDUX?" At an awards ceremony, Duffy Daugherty, then the football coach at Michigan State, told this little story. A scruffy little mongrel eagerly approached two well-coiffed poodles. "What is your name?" he asked one. Nose in the air, she said: "My name is Fifi. F-I-F-I." He put the same question to the other. Even with more disdain, she said: "My name is Mimi. M-I-M-I." The little mutt said: "Oh, yeah. Well, my name is Fido. P-H-I-D-E-A-U-X." Rod had often heard his name mispronounced or played upon but never before or after quite like that. No one in the room laughed louder than he did. (Duffy is also supposed to have said "A tie is like kissing your sister." And: "Dancing is a contact sport. Football is a collision sport.")

Rod's antics never descended to pie in the face or cream squirted from a can or gum on a cap. All of them—standard pranks in sports—fell way beneath his range of inventiveness and his comedic dignity. Nor, it should be added, did any of his players resort to such uninspired shenanigans. They knew better when he was in the vicinity. However, a clever prank pulled off with aplomb—just like clever bench-jockeying—might draw a wink from an exemplar of sly mischief. No one anywhere was outside the range of the outlandish side of the man. Ron Fairly tells about the time he and his teammates were noisily celebrating a national championship. The desk clerk called to say someone had lodged a complaint. He asked the players to "hold it down." The celebration continued as before. Elsewhere in the hotel, someone knocked on Rod's door. He opened it. He was wearing boxer shorts, socks and garters, and the red wig.

The man said: "I'm the manager of this hotel. Who is the manager of this team?"

Rod said, "I am."

The manager said, "Never mind."

Nor were solemn ceremonies inviolate. At an initiation of someone into Skull and Dagger, an honorary society, all present were assembled in front of a curtain for the presentation. The curtain parted, and a skull came forward. It was wearing the red wig.

Rod even invaded enemy territory and staked a claim to a hunk of it. San Francisco is home to a lot of Cal fans and Stanford fans. But in the midst of that bastion, on a traffic island at the corner of Columbus and Broadway in North Beach, Rod erected a sign that read "Dedeaux's Island." That slab of isolated concrete became a meeting place for USC people after a game up north. Silliness flourished. On one occasion, when John McKay, the USC football coach, was aboard the island, Rod pulled a phone from an inside pocket, handed it to McKay, and said "It's for you." Cell phones didn't exist in those days.

It might seem that Rod had two sides: one a strict coach and the other a calculating prankster and fun lover. But, in truth, his personality was all of a piece. It had many elements that worked together in myriad situations. He called upon this or that element to fit the situation, but others were always at the ready. It was as though his personality was a console with knobs he could rotate to call up what he needed. The constant was a natural upbeat temperament and a heightened sense of the moment. Fun abounded, but Rod wasn't kidding when he said "When we work, we are all business."

Serious business included intrasquad games: the starters ("the Trojans") versus the reserves ("the Spartans"). The Spartans played very hard but loosely. All the pressure was on the Trojans. No one fancied losing to the Spartans and certainly no one fancied losing his position to a Spartan. In short, these games were all-out wars. Both teams bench-jockeyed—often using insults based on inside information. No outside team knew USC's players as the Trojans and Spartans knew one another. A pitcher with a tendency for wildness might hear jungle calls from the other dugout. A batter with a tendency to strike out might hear a loud collective "swish" after he flailed at the last pitch. The rule was "anything goes." These games tested the mental toughness as much as—if not more than—games against teams outside the family. Rod saw to that.

He also tried to see to it that the Trojans won. If they were down a run or two after nine innings, he'd say: "It's still light. Let's play another inning." If the gambit didn't work, the Trojans would hear about it in the shower. "He gave you 10 innings and we still beat you." Worse, if the Trojans went ahead and won in the extra inning or two, mockery sounded through the spray. "We beat you in nine. Rod cheated for you." The Trojans won most of those games even without the gift inning but rarely without a scrap.

One of those games sticks in my memory because a participant never let me forget it. And it was memorably offbeat. That day, the Spartans decided to take things into their own hands. As they ran to their positions in the bottom of the first, Rod watched an outfielder go to shortstop, a catcher to second, an outfielder to catcher, and an infielder to left field. All were whooping and wore their caps backward. The pitcher, assigned by Rod, was a lefty who normally had trouble getting the ball over the plate. The newly minted defense and howls of defiance must have inspired him. He shut the Trojans down for five innings. Every ball the regulars hit was a routine out, even for misfit gloves. The Spartans led 2 to 0.

Rod allowed the Spartans their innovative configuration because he anticipated a good time would be had by all. Work and fun would be combined. But by the end of seven innings, the prospect of hilarity at the Spartans' expense had begun to dim. They led 3 to 0. In the bottom of the eighth, Rod called in the third pitcher for the Spartans. In the scheme of things, he functioned exclusively as a batting practice pitcher. A homer with a man on base by a Trojan power hitter made the score 3 to 2 at the end of eight. Walks and hits brought in two more runs in the bottom of the ninth. Trojans win 4 to 3. Rod insisted he brought in the third pitcher because the Spartans "had run out of arms." He also said the game showed how much depth USC had. The Spartans were "the second-best team in the league."

I remember all this because the reserve catcher who played second base that day was a lifelong best friend. His memory of school days balked on what should have been familiar details, such as graduation, but never on the time when Rod "personally chose the losing pitcher." So he said. Many times.

Trojan teams were famous for camaraderie. Did Rod risk it by promoting all-out civil war? Might not personal animosities carry over from the head knocking and dilute solidarity on game days? Rod was willing to take those risks in order to instill a competitive ethic in his players—all of them, from top to bottom on the roster. He knew that a family feud dissolves against threats from the outside. He also saw to that on game days.

Even during open tryouts, Rod looked for signs of mental toughness. The candidates were mostly a motley crew. Some wore softball jerseys. Some wore tennis shoes and T-shirts. Some wore jeans. Now and then, a kid would show up in his old high school uniform or one from amateur summer ball. True to form, Rod greeted them all cordially. They would all have a chance to run, throw, and hit. They named their positions, and Rod, wielding his magic fungo bat, started them off easy and then hit balls that might stretch even his regulars. "They have to be better than what we have." No gold gloves were discovered nor were any rifle arms. Nonetheless, Rod chattered at them encouragingly. Humiliation wasn't his style.

They all had a turn in the batter's box—against USC's best pitchers. Again, embarrassment wasn't the objective but rather a test to see who would hang in there and, perhaps, get the bat on the ball against the real thing. The real things were instructed to use their best stuff and best control.

One year, as usual, the aspirants were no match for Trojan aces—with one exception. Dick Hartunian hit "ropes" (line drives) left-handed even against a lefty with a dazzling curveball. Although an injury to his throwing arm ruled Hartunian out as a position player, he was given a uniform. Rod said, "If he can hit like that with a cold jock against our best, we can use him." During the season, Rod would point to Hartunian when a pinch hitter was needed and say, "Okay, tiger, get your gun." Dick's performance on tryout day was no fluke. He led the team in pinch-hitting. Rod had found a nugget.

I was never present when Rod dismissed the aspirants—typically all of them. But it would be like him to thank them for their time and interest and to advise them to do their best always. And it's equally probable that he enlisted a new bunch of personal fans. At least one player who didn't survive the cut at USC thanked Rod publicly for his dismissal. Rod had told him that he would be better at something other than baseball. More prophetic words were never spoken. The listener was the film producer David Wolper (*Roots, Willy Wonka & the Chocolate Factory,* and *L.A. Confidential,* among others).

More important than who to cut or who to keep on tryout day is the original recruitment of players. Rod cast a wide net. He received recommendations from coaches, friends, pro scouts, former players, and, no doubt, parents. He began with the advantage of his own reputation. Many a kid longed for the opportunity to play baseball for USC. One of them never in his wildest dreams thought that the chance would ever come. He stood 5'4" and weighed 140 pounds. He didn't play much until his senior year at Hamilton High School. He had an outstanding season. That year, the game between the city champion and the California Interscholastic Federation champion was played on the diamond at USC instead of Wrigley Field, the normal venue. Rod was in the audience. He saw the youngster make a great over-the-shoulder running catch in center field. After the game, Rod came to the dugout and sought out the youngster.

He said, "Are you the one who made that catch in center field?"

Shelly Andrens said, "Yes, sir."

Rod said, "I'd like you to come here to school."

Shelly said that just being on that diamond had made the hair stand up on his neck. Now he was actually being invited to play for USC on that field by the man himself. After Shelly's disbelief was replaced by euphoria, Rod explained all the arrangements for registration. The next time Shelly stood in center field on that diamond, he wore a USC uniform.

Rod saw a short young man make a great catch and, on that basis, offered him a scholarship to the university. He must have seen something else he liked. Certainly speed. Defense up the middle to go with his catcher and shortstop and second baseman. But also, perhaps, not just the catch but the manner in which it was made. Rod liked his players to look good, to have a certain style, to "fit" into his aesthetic as well as into his lineup. The two concepts were bound together in Rod's mind.

Obviously, his aesthetic didn't require great size or an appearance of strength and power. An All-American first baseman named Willie Ryan stood only 5'6". There have been short center fielders (such as Albie Pearson of the Angels), but a first baseman of Willie's size is a rarity at any level. Rod didn't shun pitchers who lacked an imposing physical presence on the mound. One of the best double-play combinations ever to play at USC was comprised of the Charnofsky twins—Stan and Hal—at 5'7". Art Mazmanian, an All-American second baseman, was short and slight. Many others of short stature appeared in USC lineups over the years—some of whom, perhaps, might not have been given a chance elsewhere.

The point isn't necessarily size but that Rod recruited and played young men who, as he'd say, "showed me something." He seemed to have been able to see with an inner eye that detected qualities in addition to what appears in a box score. Some people may have the paranormal in mind when they refer to Rod's "sixth sense," but more likely is that over time, he fashioned a native gift into acute perception. Sometimes, you heard that Rod got "all the best players." Kids coming out of high school aren't "the best players." They may be the best prospects or have outstanding native talent. But the jump from high school to college entails an entirely new set of challenges in athletics, in academics, and in social life. Not all gifted athletes make the transition smoothly—some not at all. Rod wasn't starved for gifted players. But that isn't the whole story. Their arrival on campus was only the beginning. In many instances, the talent was very raw. In some, the outlook needed an adjustment. Gifted people aren't invariably the easiest to teach and handle. Rod made the good ones even better and prepared many of them for professional careers, including ones whose names were later to appear on big league rosters. Others, who might have had successful careers in baseball, chose other lines of work. Rod's recruits were much improved ballplayers and better men by the time they left the university.

Rod didn't always have an all-star at every position. Some years, players that were counted on were ineligible or injured or, in the 1950s, in military service. Some players didn't perform up to expectations. Some signed pro contracts after their junior years. Some dropped out of school. Phenoms weren't always waiting in the wings. Rod filled in with less heralded players who, more often than not, "made me look good," as he'd say. (Notice that the credit goes to the player.) The man knew what to do with what was on hand.

Many of his players might have had outstanding careers at other universities and in the professional ranks. Good coaches and good baseball programs existed throughout the country. But none of the programs was as successful as the one Rod ran. He constructed an environment of success that increased the chances of success for individuals. They played with and for and off one another. This dynamic was at the center of the program. His lineup was made with this matching of strengths in mind. Players fit. That might have also happened if they had gone to another university. One can only speculate. At USC, the record obviates the urge even to wonder mildly. It's pointless, really, to say something like: "He would have been just as good if he'd gone to X. He had that much talent." No one knows. I was discussing with a scout one of our pitchers he was interested in. He said: "Around here, they should be polished after playing for Rod. I look for that."

Polish was applied to Tom Seaver in what he calls his "journey to the big leagues." Within two years of his 1965 season at USC, he was the winning pitcher in the 1967 All-Star game. Seaver credits Don Appleby, his coach in Babe Ruth baseball, with launching that journey. He recalls that after high school, he moved in 1963 from reserve to active status in the U.S. Marine corps for six months—three of them in boot camp. ("Once a Marine, a Marine forever.") He pitched at Fresno City College in 1964 and then transferred to USC. By that time, he had taken several steps on his journey. The timing was perfect for Rod Dedeaux to enter the picture. Seaver was at his last pre-professional step. Rod, he says, taught him "intellectual enthusiasm" and "controlled emotion." His confidence grew because Rod "gave me the ball when it was my turn." Like others, he came to believe that if Rod thinks I can, I can.

In that 1967 All-Star came, Seaver was a rookie—"the last man on the roster" and the only pitcher left for the National League when the game went into extra innings. He was, he says, "scared to death." But once on the mound, facing a powerful American League lineup, he summoned the attitude he had learned from Rod: "I can do this." He even broke an old rule of thumb: Don't put the tying or winning run on base. He instead chose another path: Don't let their big man beat you. The big man was Carl Yastrzemski, who was on his way to winning the last Triple Crown in baseball before Miguel Cabrera won it in 2012. Seaver said, "I walked him on four pitches, then struck the next guy out on three pitches." He was the winning pitcher.

The Seaver Story (or "journey," in his words) illustrates Rod's impact on superior talent. Seaver might have won 300 games and have been elected to the Hall of Fame if he had never met Rod Dedeaux. But he took the last big step into the big leagues outfitted with a state of mind that he credits Rod with instilling. We can't know what else might have happened, but we do know what happened. For it, we have Tom Seaver's word. He came to USC ready for the finishing touches. Polish—and more—was waiting for him.

Managing the Game

Football coaches call every play. Basketball coaches run up and down the sidelines yelling instructions. (If they pause to tie a shoe, when they look up, a 10-point turnaround could have occurred.) Hockey coaches try not to fall too far behind. Baseball managers and coaches appear only to make strange movements with their hands. But good ones, such as Rod, are enmeshed in the game as much as a conductor of a symphony. All that has been said about his verbal skills might leave the impression he gave rousing pep talks before a game. Not so. He avoided the clichés of sports combat. He didn't sermonize. He didn't speak in mottoes or plaster them on the walls of the locker room. He neither pleaded nor provoked his players to grow ravenous for victory. He didn't come equipped with any form of adrenaline pump. He believed that inspiration comes from preparation. He went methodically over the strengths and weaknesses of the opposing lineup by using information gathered from a network of ex-players or pals now coaching in high school or in community college, from scouts, and from cronies—to all of which were added his own direct observations. On some players, he had virtually a complete book. On others, maybe he had only a few scraps, and on still others, he had almost nothing. Of the last, he'd say, "Let's watch batting and infield practice and first time through their order."

By then, he was ready to peg them. These assessments weren't crude or of the one-size-fits-all variety. Approach to hitters was guided by what our pitcher did best in relation to a specific batter. Rod might say "Challenge him" or, conversely, "Don't throw him a fastball in the strike zone." Even the latter might be amended if the hitter was set up looking for a change-up or a breaking ball, and Rod had confidence his pitcher wouldn't groove one. Adjustments were made during the game. The skull session laid the floor plan and arranged the furniture but didn't nail it down. The pitcher and catcher sat next to Rod in the dugout, and all three were in constant communication.

Nowadays, I have the impression that many college coaches send the pitch calls to their catchers. Rod might give advice or even specific instructions between innings, but he knew that the young man behind the plate was in the best spot to know what was or wasn't getting batters out. By and large, the catcher called the pitches. Rod was always teaching young men to embrace and handle responsibility. That attitude even extended to the student manager. Gary Shimokawa, who held that position from 1962 to 1964, says that Rod "let me do my job … but always would consult with me on what was going on … how to pay the umpires, what bats to use during BP or intrasquad games … saving the better equipment for our regular lineup. Even who rubbed up the baseballs … I often did them for the umpires." Rod stayed in touch with what Gary was doing but didn't look over his shoulder. Note the term *consult*. Once a job was defined, the person was trusted to carry it out according to plan—down to the last detail.

Rod also explained how the defense would play every batter—at least to start with. Adjustments were made if necessary. Prospective bunters were identified, as were guys who liked to hit the other way. He had special instructions for dealing with players who were itchy to steal. Of some, he'd say: "Likes to run but can't. Lull him a little. He'll go and we'll nail him." (Sort of a gift out.) Of those who had good speed, he'd say: "Let him get a lead. Hold the ball. Then, step off the rubber. Look him back to first. Maybe show him a couple of commercials [soft tosses]. Then, if he gets too big a lead, give him your best shot. Never throw to home if he's got too big a lead or is moving toward second. Cut his lead and make him stand still." All these instructions might read like a page from Pitching 101. But they're often observed more in the breach than in practice by professionals. Rod figured that larceny on the base paths was a Trojan birthright. A steal by an opponent was a violation of the natural order. "If they're going to advance a runner, make them bunt and give up an out."

He worked at the analytic and intuitive levels and had a feel for the evolving rhythm of a contest. Thus, he was able to anticipate what turns the game might take. (Not predict. Baseball is too nutty for that.) He said, "You always have to think two or three innings down the road." That he did, even if one team jumped out early to what looked like a commanding lead. If the opponent jumped out, Rod would look unfazed and, I think, was unfazed. He was alert to flaws or chinks in the other side that ultimately might be exploited. In one game, when the opposing pitcher had a no-hitter for three innings, he said: "He's too comfortable. He's getting too many first-pitch called strikes on fastballs." The conventional wisdom in that situation, with your club already down four runs, calls for "making the guy pitch" by waiting him out a bit. (Today, it would be called running up the pitch count.) But Rod told his batters to step into the box ready to pull the trigger on the first good pitch they saw. In the fourth inning, USC's bats came alive, spurred by two hits on first pitches. In the fifth inning, the opposing pitcher, a little shell shocked, grew more cautious and walked a couple of batters. He was in the shower before the inning ended.

Once he had the lead, Rod escalated the pressure with stolen bases and hit-and-run plays. USC won going away. His starter settled down after a rocky first couple of innings but was eventually lifted when his day's work was satisfactorily completed. Rod would rather lose money in the stock market than lose a lead in a baseball game. He liked things the other way around. He was called "the Houdini of Bovard" because his teams so often came from behind to win—frequently in the last two innings or in the bottom of the ninth. He was Yogi before Yogi came along. "It ain't over till it's over."

The most dramatic instance occurred in an elimination game at the 1973 College World Series. The Trojans trailed Minnesota 7-0 in the bottom of the ninth. Dave Winfield (yes, *that* Dave Winfield) had already struck out 15 Trojans. The outlook for a comeback couldn't have been bleaker, except for the coach and players faced with the challenge. Rod kept saying "Let's win this one." Fans had begun to leave the stadium, but many returned when the radio reported that USC was pecking away at what seemed like an insurmountable lead. The man who had fanned 15 suddenly couldn't put the Trojans away. Nor could his relief on the mound. USC scored eight runs and was given a standing ovation by an astounded crowd.

But USC, always the top dog, was booed the following night when they took the field against Arizona State for the championship. A tribute to an historic victory had an abbreviated shelf life. The boos were wasted. In another barn burner and with another comeback, the Trojans prevailed in 13 innings.

In a reverse situation, in 1948, the Trojans led Yale by one run in the ninth inning of the College World Series championship game. Yale loaded the bases with no one out. Rod went to the mound and said to players gathered there, "This is the way we like it." Everyone laughed. The batter hit a line drive that resulted in a triple play. (Rod said later that he'd put the sign on for that play.) USC won its first of 11 national titles. The on deck batter before the triple play was George H. W. Bush, the Yale first baseman and captain and future president of the United States. He said of himself, "Good field, no hit." But no one knows what might have happened if he'd had a chance to swing the bat that day.

Although he was a war hero, George Bush wasn't a famous opponent. Rod liked to test famous opponents early in a game, especially pitchers. You didn't want them to settle in and establish supremacy. You tried to get them off their game. To shake their confidence. One of them was named Brad Tolson, a senior, who was completing a brilliant career at the University of Arizona. We went to Tucson by train and tried to sleep the night before the game in a makeshift dorm beneath the football stadium. Concrete had absorbed heat all day and released it on us at night. We took the field the next night not in the mood to act the good guest. The stadium was packed with rambunctious fans. Arizona wasn't at the time a member of what later would become the Pac-10. But their players and fans had visions of Tolson leading the desert outliers to victory over the gilded invaders. He was riding a 17-game winning streak, his team a 20-game streak.

The best-laid plans, as they say. Rod said: "He likes to get ahead with first-pitch fastballs. Go right after him." I don't recall how many hits USC put together in the first couple of innings—some of them on first-pitch fastballs. Tolson insisted on coming back with the fastball if the first pitch missed. Neither he nor the catcher nor the coach altered the pattern. He was sticking with his trusted recipe for success. He got shelled. And looked it. And heard about it from our dugout. He lasted only two innings. The stadium was quiet.

Rod primed his team to attack an ace pitcher on the road in a hostile environment. The crowd was taken out of the game early. It was the biggest game of the year for Arizona. For Rod, every game was the biggest game. We had a meal, returned to our concrete oven under the stadium, and, drained of adrenaline, collapsed. (Enough energy was left to bellow wisecracks about the game.) The Trojans left on the field that night everything they'd brought to Tucson, and lost 9-2 the next day.

Rod wanted badly to win that first game to keep the upstarts in their place. He didn't talk like that or act like that. But we understood the stakes. Plant your flag in the territory of an enemy that aspires to upset what was in his mind the natural order of the baseball universe. If you have this mindset, you will overcome such adverse conditions as unusual heat, bad digs, an ace pitcher, and a tough crowd eager to celebrate your demise. He didn't anticipate or warn against adversity or quirks. You took them in stride. His teams often played in circumstances that wouldn't have been mistaken for a warm bath of comfort or a semblance of familiarity. At one point, the UCLA home park was Joe E. Brown Field. It was vast and windswept and had no fences. Balls hit into the gaps could roll forever. Balls that would have departed any stadium in America surrendered meekly to the wind and were caught. The field in Berkeley had no left field fence. Right field ended in the concrete back of a track stadium. Cal fans misbehaved. (Someone threw a tennis ball at me while I was warming up to start.) Santa Clara fans were even worse. During one game, they slipped a hose into the USC dugout and turned the water on. I seem to recall that Santa Clara's home park had a skin infield. The Sunken Diamond at Stanford felt like an island in the middle of nowhere. An incline in front of the left field wall added an obstacle for the outfielder. Compared to these venues, Bovard Field—even with its idiosyncrasies—was an honest baseball park.

The idea of hospitality didn't come immediately to mind in some of the visitors' locker rooms, where, as the old joke says, you had to go outside to change your mind. Or in "free" digs. In a sports barracks at Camp Pendleton, we shared space with a Marine boxing team. They hurled obscene verbal hooks at one another until the officer of the day shouted "Knock it off." By then, it was probably two in the morning. (We did learn some creative dirty words.) Their baseball team included pro players who had joined the Marines to avoid being drafted into the army. The commanding officer of the base "requested their presence "as soon as he saw their names on the rolls of new inductees. Not to put too fine a point on it, but that team was loaded. They beat us in a close game.

In Rod's mind, conditions should be psychologically irrelevant unless they're advantageous. He might have adapted to dimensions on the field but would brook no excuses for mental lapses or distractions owing to unfriendly or quirky or uncomfortable environments. Certainly not to the jeering of fans, who reserved special invective for the Trojans. He expected the same level of concentration everywhere. A loss was more likely to be attributed to defects in our performance than to what we were taught to consider extraneous factors. He always put primary responsibility on his players. By taking responsibility, Rod didn't mean that players should mope around for days under a cloud of shame or blame but that people who believe they can be masters of their own fate try hard to bend fate to their wills. They may be acting on an illusion but a functional one, especially in sports.

Rod didn't make too much or too little of unusual hazards. He took them into account if they might affect the outcome of a game. He didn't accuse other teams of cheating or placing booby traps in his path. He didn't disparage other coaches or authorities at their universities. He was more than ready—even pleased—to take on what came with being on top. Opposing fans paid no attention to mediocre visitors. To Rod, their taunting was a sign of respect. In short, he primed his players to win—whatever the conditions and wherever the contest.

Rod knew he'd lose some, but he never capitulated in his mind, even when the baseball gods were cackling at him. None of his players ever capitulated in their minds either. Signs of a "dobber down" would earn a quick trip to the bench. Such signs, I would guess, were very rare during his tenure as head coach. Indeed, he didn't have to give fire-and-brimstone or happy-talk sermons before games because anyone he thought needed that sort of artificial uplift in order to give his best at all times wouldn't have been in the room anyway.

Rod played for the big inning. He'd rather try to advance a runner by hitting to the right side than by bunting and giving up an out. Even pitchers who could handle the bat were given a chance to "take a shot." "Balls go through a shuffling defense." In batting practice, players used the last swing in a set to practice hitting the ball to the opposite field. But Rod would rather get a bunch. Like Earl Weaver, he was greatly attached to the three-run homer. He followed this power program more at home than on the road—in part because right field at old Bovard Field had a short porch. He recruited lefty power to exploit the cozy dimensions. But he didn't completely abandon the program on the road. "It's important to stay on top on the road to neutralize the home field advantage," as in Tucson. He didn't disbelieve the old adage "play to tie on the road" by bunting late in the game, but he wasn't a slave to it. As always, judgment was based on circumstances. Who's at the plate for us? How's the defense set? How much speed do we have on the bases? Maybe a steal instead of a bunt. How has their pitcher been going?

Even behind late in a game on the road, Rod was reluctant to abandon a push for a big inning—a sudden killer punch in the last round, so to speak. Other coaches, aware of his unpredictability, couldn't confidently settle on a defensive maneuver. Usually, they went by the book to stymie him, but he could be on another page. He might give the sign for a steal or a hit-and-run when USC was behind if he had the right men on base and at the plate. Players could attempt a steal on their own, especially of third base. But when Rod was giving this permission, he'd say in the voice that hinted of exile in a frigid climate: "But you have to make it, tiger."

In a game I attended many years after graduation, USC trailed by one run with one out in the bottom of the ninth inning and had a runner on second. The second baseman and shortstop were playing deep in order to knock down any ball going into the outfield, which would have allowed the runner to score. They paid scant attention to the runner. Neither bird-dogged him. (Feinted toward the base in order to shorten his lead off the bag.) On the first pitch, the pitcher took a cursory glance at the runner and hurriedly threw to the plate. On the second pitch, the runner took a big sashaying lead, got a rolling start, and stole third easily. He did what he'd been taught to do: size up the situation and then execute flawlessly. Now the infield was forced to play in tight to cut the run off at the plate. The batter looped a hit that might have been caught by the shortstop had he been in his regular position. The Trojans won the game in the 10th inning.

Maybe the defense and the pitcher failed to follow their coach's instructions—if they'd been instructed—because the second baseman and shortstop feared that a hit would go through if they were busy bird-dogging the runner and the pitcher was concentrating entirely on the batter. If the tables had been turned, Rod would have fined the pitcher and both infielders had they acted as the opposition did that day. The man on second must not be permitted to get a big lead—and certainly not be in motion toward third. The pitcher should step off the rubber and walk toward the runner while at least one infielder runs to the bag. The runner is shown that everyone is keeping an eye on him. If necessary, the process is repeated until the runner's lead is reduced and he's standing still. The shortstop can also give the sign for a pickoff play. Even if it fails to nip the runner, he still gets the message: Don't wander too far from the base and plant your puppies. Better still: Lean back toward second just to be on the safe side. Afterward, Rod said that the runner had gone on his own. What if he'd been thrown out at third? Rod winked and said, "He wasn't." If you don't brood over spilt milk, you certainly don't imagine spilt milk. We live in the present tense.

Rod didn't harass or nag umpires. If he thought an ump had missed a pitch, he might yell "Where was that pitch?" or "Bring the ball down." And let it go at that. But he never missed an opportunity to massage an ump for doing "the right thing" for our side. He never resorted to anything as crude as a cheer or an explicit compliment. On a day when Pacific Coast League umpire Hank Soar (a former NFL star who caught the game-winning touchdown pass in the 1938 NFL Championship Game against the Green Bay Packers, giving the New York Giants their third NFL title) was giving me the low strike, Rod yelled, "Stay right there, Davie." To Hank, this meant, indirectly, "You're doing a great job. Keep it up." But to Ralph Coleman, the coach in the Oregon State dugout, it meant "My batters will keep getting screwed." He started barking at Soar early in the game and kept it up. He drew a few stern looks, but Soar wasn't inclined to eject him from a game that would decide the championship of the Pacific Coast Conference and a trip to Omaha for the College World Series.

Not inclined up to a point. That point came in the seventh inning, when a ball got away from their catcher and a runner scored from third. Our batter pointed in the wrong direction for the ball, and their catcher duly followed the false lead. While he was looking for the phantom ball, our runner, who had started on second, kept coming and also scored. The catcher exploded. He'd been deceived. Coleman had had enough. He raced to the plate and harangued Soar about, of all things, "that dirty trick." He stomped around. He looked foolish—a small man with a mustache like that of Ronald Colman, the movie star, doing an angry dance and hurling insults at a man the size of a bull. Finally, Soar said calmly: "That's it. You're out of here." Coleman sputtered: "You can't do that. I've never been kicked out of a game in my life." Soar, now with a voice like a foghorn, said, "Well, Coley, you go back to Corvallis and report that you lost your virginity in Los Angeles." Coleman shuffled off without a peep.

Rod certainly couldn't have envisioned this outcome when he was petting Soar. He'd later say: "Coley is a good guy. I'd never seen him like that." As if he'd had nothing to do with it—even slightly. Soar was probably going to keep calling that borderline pitch a strike no matter what. But it never hurts to hear that you're doing a good job.

Unlike Coleman, Clint Evans, then the coach at Cal, wasn't known for a serene exterior. He'd rag on umpires and call his players out loudly during games. If they were swinging when they should have been taking, he'd forgo hand signs and yell "Take!" so everyone in the park could hear. To make sure, he might sit in a folding chair near the batter's box. On this day, our batter ran into fair territory after an overthrow at first. The catcher, who'd backed up the play, made a lunge to tag the runner but missed and fell flat on his face. The runner tiptoed back to first safely. Clint sprinted across the diamond from the third base dugout, hollering, "Dammit, Tilly, here we go again." Tilly Schafer was a fixture among umpires on ball fields in Southern California. Clint was short and wiry and was gesticulating to show how his catcher had made the tag. The catcher didn't complain. He knew he'd missed. But Clint was in no mood to ask him. Nor did he get anywhere with Tilly. Then, he did something that was rare if not unheard of. He took his complaint to the opposing coach. He hitched up his pants and strode toward the USC dugout. "C'mon, Rod. Dammit. Every time I come down here, this guy screws me. He's been doin' it for years. You know it. You keep hirin' him. Give me a break." This must have been one of the few times in Rod's life that he was speechless. Tilly rescued him. "Clint, you've had your say. Get back in the dugout or I'll run you." Clint threw up his hands and did a pigeon walk back to the dugout to the cheers of the crowd. He actually was a good man and a good coach but perhaps a little excitable. In 1947, his team won the national championship in the first College World Series.

Just as Ted Williams got the benefit of close calls, Rod probably did too, especially at home. This isn't to say that the umpires were homers, but they were human. Life isn't fair. Rod didn't want a game to be fair. He wanted every break he could get. His teams were famous for seizing the moment when they got a break. In those days, Rod scheduled midweek games with some of the smaller colleges in Southern California. They had nothing to lose and showed up giddy with thoughts of an upset. On this day, Pepperdine was getting all the breaks. Bloopers dropped in. A ball that our third baseman was about to field hit the bag. The umpire missed a call at first and two of their runners scored. Their pitcher threw a lot of soft stuff, and the Trojans were overswinging. Rod was more perplexed than fazed. He'd often said, "Don't let them stay close enough to think they can win." Now they were ahead by five runs in the seventh inning.

He paced the dugout, clapping his hands and saying "It's time, tigers." USC started putting runners on base until the bases were loaded. In the meantime, Pepperdine had recorded two outs. The batter hit an easy ground ball to third that would have ended the inning and perhaps decided the game. But the third baseman booted the ball. Before the third out was recorded, USC had scored seven runs and added two more in the eighth. The error was a break—a big one—and as usual, USC capitalized on it. But in Rod's mind, the pressure on the other team had finally told. He believed it would happen sooner or later. Often enough, it did.

To Rod, a baseball game was like a work of art. You made a frame and a sketch and then went to work seriously. You looked closely. You stepped back for perspective. You added the right touch to impose balance or imbalance where the one would be the more effective. You applied a strong stroke here or a dabble there. You visualized the overall desired complexion and strove for it. You didn't have total control of the finished product, as a painter does, but with imagination and reason, you could exert more control than someone who simply stared at the canvas or waited dumbly for a jolt from the muse. He said in one of our conversations: "You can't always keep a game from getting out of hand or put the other team away. But if there's any chance to and you don't, you shouldn't be in charge." Time and again, he made the right move at the right time—often a surprising move—that altered the complexion to satisfy his design. He was lucky at times, but as he said, "Luck is the residue of design." This compact statement underscored the importance of preparation.

Rod was a gambler, a hunch player, even a guesser, but not without a basis. His mind was like a computer—a huge repository of information capable of making instantaneous connections. (Fifteen years or more after your graduation, he'd introduce you to a couple of his current players and recall an incident that made you look good.) He might have seemed bold and daring, and in a sense, he was—but with calculation not always limited to the percentages. He had comprehensive ideas about baseball, but they were guidelines, not an ironclad framework. On game day, he was flexible and nimble with strategy and tactics.

He was also on patrol duty. Among other things, the message was: "You never know when you'll be needed. You're not here to spectate." If you have a uniform, even if you haven't played an inning, you might be in the game at any minute. Be ready when your chance comes. It might come only once. Up and down the bench, he traveled, stopping to comment on what had just happened. "See, tigers, we can't allow the extra base. The throw was off line. That's a mental mistake." The tone of remarks like this was rarely combative. The words came deliberately in a low register, accompanied by a frown. Mistakes hurt the man. Rod didn't rattle off instructional details when making these remarks. He reminded but didn't literally teach on the bench. Too much thinking in the midst of battle can distract the mind.

Usually, Rod made comments when he was on a trip to or from the fine pad. It was attached to a clipboard that hung above his place in the dugout. Fines ranged from a nickel to a quarter depending on the severity and timing of the offense. As judge and jury, Rod enjoyed much latitude in handing down penalties. Pure equity wasn't always honored. A mistake that routinely cost 15 cents might be bumped up to a quarter if the judge was sufficiently upset. Absolute power implies flexibility. Or whimsicality. Rod was human. A catalogue of offenses includes the following:

- Grammar (profanity on the field or in the dugout)
- Head in the stands (checking for the girlfriend, parents, friends, scouts, or a cutie for later)
- Inactivity on the bench (no lethargy or daydreaming allowed)
- Missing a sign (and possibly messing up a play)
- Failure to get a bunt down ("There is no excuse.")
- Alphonse and Gaston* ("Communicate and never let a ball drop between two or three of you.")
- Bad throw (in any and all situations, including infield practice before a game. "It makes the team look bad. No one's running. There's time to make a perfect throw.")
- Failure to give a good target (the relay and the cutoff man)
- Failure to set up on a direct line (the relay and the cutoff man)
- Picked off base (runner and coach)
- Doubled up on a line drive (a cardinal sin)
- Failure to touch a base while running ("Get your pace right.")
- Failure to tag up and score from third (runner and coach)
- Running into an out unnecessarily (at least get into a rundown)
- Thrown out at third on a ball hit in front of you ("Make the ball go through.")
- Thrown out at third with less than two outs (but exceptions were made)
- Mildly assenting to a tag at the plate (no rough stuff, but at least try to dislodge the ball or upend the catcher)
- Not knowing how many outs there are ("Wake up and smell the coffee.")
- Walking the other pitcher (no freebies to weak bats, but make sure he can't hurt you)
- Pitcher not covering first on a ground ball to the right side (a cardinal sin)
- Wildness out of the pen ("Throw strikes during warm-up on the mound and keep throwing them.")
- Making too good a pitch on 0 and 2 ("Don't let him off the hook when he's yours.")
- Pitcher not backing up at third or home ("What else have you got to do?")
- Botching a pickoff play (a pitcher missing the sign or, worse, throwing to an unprotected base when no sign was given)
- Pitcher throwing to the plate with an infielder out of position
- Bad jump on a fly ball (after all those drills!—but exceptions were made)
- Out of position to make a play (after all those drills!—or, worse, "Didn't you see me wave to you?")
- Taking too many hittable pitches ("Be ready to pull the trigger, tiger.")

*Alphonse and Gaston were comic strip characters from the early 1900s who were known for being polite yet clumsy.

- Chasing too many bad pitches ("Don't help their pitcher.")
- Failure to advance a runner by hitting to the right side (but exceptions were made)
- Dobber down (no tolerance for even a hint of defeatism)
- Not hustling (rarely needed but costly)
- Hotdogging or other forms of showmanship (bad form, and costly)

The official name of the fine pad was Bovard Boners. The first boner of the day cost the offender a buck. In addition to this standard catalogue, Rod would assess impromptu penalties, such as the time he fined a catcher for going behind the plate without his mask ("We try to protect ourselves at all times") or the time he fined a third base coach for bobbling an easy dribbler ("Charge the ball"). The exceptions referred to weren't made in the spirit of leniency but only if conditions somehow interfered with "the right play." Otherwise, you were docked. Rod wore a severe robe.

After a victory came the ritual singing of "McNamara's Band." (Rod said he got the idea after hearing Dennis Day sing the song on a Jack Benny program.) After a defeat, Rod always said "We'll get 'em next time." I never saw him show deep disappointment either to his team or to his assistants in the coaches' quarters. He might have been depressed—even stunned—by a tough loss, especially one traceable to a bad break, a bad call, or a freakish play, but it wasn't in his temperament to brood or to remain anchored in the past. He was the ultimate realist. "That's baseball," he'd say, and he meant it.

His pragmatism and poise were most dramatically tested, perhaps, in 1953. That club had only five seniors: the outfielders, the other starting pitcher, and me. It was our first year as regular starters. The outfielders weren't three-year starters. The catcher and all four infielders were sophomores. We weren't a seasoned outfit. It took half a season for us to come together and make a run at Stanford in first place. We caught them and finished in a dead heat. Rod said that if necessary, the playoff could be held in Palo Alto under street lamps. But Stanford pleaded preparation for final exams. Rod said: "They heard our feet coming. They want no part of us now." He had no choice but to agree to the flip of a coin.

The team assembled in the varsity locker room while Rod was on the phone with the commissioner of the conference and the Stanford coach. We had trouble believing the method of resolution. We had even more trouble believing the result but knew it as soon as Rod entered the room. "Rack 'em up," he said, looking not so much disappointed as chilled. He said a few words about our great comeback season and made the rounds to make sure his players kept their heads up. We thought: "OK, that's baseball, but this isn't. This is absurd." And so did he in his heart, as I learned when the subject came up years later.

Rod did one of his best coaching jobs with that team. He'd lost his entire infield and three starting pitchers from 1952. The catcher was a sophomore handling two pitchers who were regular starters for the first time. But from day one, Rod acted as if the best college players in the world comprised his roster. He gave us seniors explicit responsibility for leadership. He didn't alter either his attitude or his teaching style. If he considered the season a "bridge year," he never let on to the players. He didn't hurry or press players to develop at an unnatural pace. He was very patient. All the younger players seemed to "get it" at once. The race was on. The club went on a tear for the remainder of the season. Its collective personality verged on glee.

A flip of a coin denied Rod the ultimate reward of a trip to Omaha. He and the players deserved at least one last chance to prove that USC was the right team to represent the conference. How that team would have fared in the College World Series can't be known. But it had become more and more aware of its qualities and its possibilities as the season progressed. It was ready for the biggest challenge. And wanted it.

Always on Monday, first thing, he gathered the troops at the mound. There, he reviewed the good, the bad, and the ugly of the weekend. Praise was given mostly for attitude and heads-up play. He singled out "right plays," especially if one of them had undeniably affected the outcome. "You see, Hal takes that extra base, scores on the sacrifice fly, and we win by one."

Then, he'd pick up the fine pad. Most players already knew they were on it because it was purposefully in full view in the dugout. Players didn't fear this moment. No one would leave with a mark of shame on his forehead. The purpose of the exercise was, as always, teaching, not embarrassment. But occasionally, his voice would drop into lugubrious accents, as if in disbelief that a player of his could pull such a boner. "See, tigers, we can't ..." Even during what was, after all, a recitation of criticism, Rod would interject light observations. The mistake itself might not have been funny, but if a player had looked goofy, Rod could mimic the event with cruel accuracy.

Conclusion

Rod's belief in the power of positive thinking wasn't naive. In itself, it can't bring success. It's the result of success. Self-esteem follows rather than precedes achievement. You have to believe in yourself, but you must have good reasons to believe in yourself. He taught his players how to earn those reasons. It isn't enough to know. Ultimate confidence arrives when you know that you know. That depends, in turn, on accomplishments that come from "playing the game right." Rod taught not only what to do and how to do it but why it should be done that way. The "why" glued all the parts together.

Nor did he think that phony heroics or infantile strutting are reliable methods of intimidation. In his scheme, razzing the opposition and maintaining composure were elements in a program of intimidation, but unless they were anchored in crisp and intelligent performance, they were just noise and theater that didn't deserve to be taken seriously. You had to earn the right to pop off and to carry your head high. Otherwise, you were relying on superficial gimmicks. His program dug deep beneath the surface, where everything comes together in tough-minded integrity.

I repeat that Rod was an amiable perfectionist. He stressed punctuality at the start and alertness and determination until the end. If the bus was scheduled to leave for the airport at 8 a.m., at eight on the dot, he'd say, "Roll 'em, bussy." Players who showed up at 8:01 were left behind. He enforced a strict dress code on the road and on the field, and players weren't allowed to wear any part of uniform gear on campus. Gray T-shirts that read "Property of USC Athletics" were meant to go under uniforms, not to impress girls at the statue of Tommy Trojan or in the cafeteria. Game hats were shaped properly. Spikes were buffed. Uniform pants were worn halfway at the calf. No long stirrups to reveal too much sanitary stocking. And definitely no pants drooping down over spikes. (That look wasn't in fashion then anyway.) Uniforms were folded into traveling bags to minimize wrinkling. Coats and ties or USC traveling shirts were required on planes, in restaurants, and in hotels.

"We go first class," he said. That term signified everything about baseball and about conduct in general. It applied less to money (although he said "it only costs a dime more to go first class") than to attitude and demeanor. It was part of a larger program of indoctrination to make players feel they were special. He might say, "It's great to be a Trojan" or "It's great to be on a winner." Or he might say to a bus driver: "Whack it, bussy. You're driving a winner." But I never heard him say that players should feel honored or grateful to be included in "the Trojan family." (I can't say flatly, of course, that he never uttered the sentiment.) Again, that sort of language wasn't his style. The message was implicit in his teaching, his expectations, and, not least, in his own actions and speech. Nor did I ever hear him say that he was "honored to coach such a fine bunch of young men." Or anything close to it. He never patronized his players. He manipulated them (it's called coaching), but he wasn't condescending. He wasn't given to expressing gaudy sentiments. From him, the word *appreciate* said it all. Even when he was complimenting a player, any impulse to gush was held in check. A straightforward compliment was enough from him. His players knew it.

They also knew that on public occasions, he was always a threat to exploit for laughs one of their less glorious moments. At a banquet, he giggled all the way through a story about the USC pitcher in a game at the College World Series who hit the player he was trying to pick off first base. The man stole second. The pitcher whirled to pick him off second and plunked him again. The man stole third. The pitcher made a feint to pick him off third. "I went to the mound and took the ball before he killed someone." He could adapt an old gag to the occasion: "Billy Doyle was the slowest player I ever saw. I set up a foot race between him and a pregnant woman. Billy finished third." Or about a pitcher he spotted in the audience: "They used to say when it was his turn, 'Come early if you want to see the starting pitcher.'"

Discipline in sports comes in many forms. At one extreme are coaches who yell a lot and take punitive measures. At the other are coaches who tread quietly and are tight-lipped. Rod was neither. He didn't holler at players. He didn't punish dramatically or publicly. He used as few or as many words as necessary. He had no gimmicks. What he did have was the knack of scolding without seeming to. That attribute wasn't entirely a function of his temperament. He believed it was the best way to handle young men. Nor was seeming to feel betrayed by mistakes only a matter of heart. It was a motivational tool. He knew his players hated to let him down. Everyone wanted to please him. Everyone wanted his approval.

Without any shows of ego or self-aggrandizement, Rod was aware of his stature and its impact on his players. He did nothing out of the ordinary to gain respect, except to be extraordinary. Like all good coaches, he enjoyed it personally, although I never heard him mention it. In all our conversations, I never heard him say anything like "You have to make your players respect you." You gained that by doing your job well. Any job.

That lesson is one of many that players took from their experience under him. Don't lust after praise. Don't show off. Don't sulk. If you've got the goods, the right people will notice. Don't take shortcuts. You won't get there any faster or with the right preparation. And you will probably have to go back over missed ground while others are getting ahead. Pay attention to everything. The "insignificant" detail is the one that will trip you up in the end. Above all, be patient and wait for your chance. Be ready. It may come only once. That last point is worth repeating, as this book has emphasized. It was Rod's supreme lesson for life.

3

His Legacy

Rod's legacy is lodged foremost in the history of Trojan baseball. His record of 11 national championships, 28 conference championships, and victories in seven games out of 10 will probably never be surpassed. It would be a remarkable record in any sport. In baseball, it reduces the odds to shambles. The record is frozen in time. The lineage continues.

When Stan Charnofsky was the baseball coach at San Fernando Valley State College (now California State University at Northridge), his assistant was Dick Enberg. In time, Dick left teaching and coaching to become a broadcaster, and he's currently the play-by-play announcer for the San Diego Padres. Dick has said on more than one occasion that he learned all he knows about baseball from Stan, one of Rod's prize pupils. Rod's baseball knowledge spread from the diamond to the airwaves.

But on the diamond is where the lineage has had the most influence. Many of Rod's players went on to coach in high school or in a community college, and he was succeeded at USC by Mike Gillespie, one of his own. In turn, the players they coached joined the coaching ranks. Three members of a state championship team I coached in Coalinga, California, transferred to universities and had outstanding careers and then became high school coaches. After completing his A.A. degree in Coalinga, Mickey McNamee played for Rod at USC. Jim Harper played at Cal Poly at San Luis Obispo, where he was the captain in his senior year. To his delight, he exchanged lineup cards with Rod at home plate before a game against the Trojans. Max Culp finished his college career at the University of Nevada at Reno. All three said they applied to their coaching what they had learned from me—in a direct line from the master. In turn, several of their players became coaches. And on and on. It never ends. The game has changed in some ways and each coach has a unique personality, but the principles, attitudes, and methods that Rod taught are timeless.

It's bracing to consider that we were and are in a lineage that began, according to Rod himself, with Casey Stengel. Looking back, Casey said that the most knowledgeable baseball man and best teacher he ever played for was John McGraw with the New York Giants from 1921 to 1923. In baseball generations, Casey was son to McGraw, Rod grandson to McGraw, Rod's players great-grandsons to McGraw, our players … It's not entirely fanciful to think that important lessons were passed along the pipeline from one man to another. Casey, of course, had his own ideas, as did Rod and all of us, and we all related to players and presented information in our own styles. Information is shaped and colored by personality. But DNA instilled by great teachers has a long life and lasting influence, even if not consciously.

No claim is made that men in this lineage possessed the "secret knowledge" of a mystical cult that denied membership to all other baseball players, coaches, and managers. But the decisive factor is how knowledge is communicated, how its nuances are explained, how it's directed to individuals, and how it plays in action during games. In short, how it's articulated so all its parts make sense in relation to one another. At that point, it becomes "second nature," as Rod would say. The learner possesses it and is possessed by it and can't even imagine not only a better way but any other way at all. Because it works.

All of us in the wide, wide world beyond the diamond should have taken from Rod lessons about life that were implicit in how he coached the team and treated us as individuals. The main one, as I've already said, is doing things right and being ready when your chance comes. Of equal value is trusting a person to whom you've given responsibility. Rod set expectations but didn't breathe over your shoulder. If you delivered the goods when your chance came, he tended to stick with you. More than anything, he wanted you to succeed—for his sake, for the team's sake, and for your own. He communicated this managerial outlook especially when he was expressing criticism in order to keep trust in the forefront. You didn't fear that the axe would fall at the slightest misstep. He knew how to gin up alertness without causing jumpiness. He made changes and replaced players, of course, as all coaches do when necessary, but he didn't make them hastily. While you were in place, he made you feel that you were the best man for the job. After all, he was trusting you to help maintain the status of the best baseball program in the country. Pressure inhered in these circumstances, but it was the kind that every USC player longed for and embraced. It meant you had arrived.

Randy Johnson, who had a brilliant career in the major leagues for 22 seasons, singles out Rod's understanding of "where his players were coming from." He says that Rod gave him an "opportunity to sink or swim at the college level." Rod was "very patient" with Randy, as he was with all players who showed they possessed the right qualities to play baseball at USC.

Rod was able to intuit when the player being given a chance was ready. He seemed to know who was prepared for the test. If you had any sense, you knew he knew. In itself, this knowledge was a confidence booster. You were picked for a job by a man who didn't pick just anybody. You still had to pass the test. But it helped enormously that he thought you were the man of the moment and that he'd select the right moment. The occasion wasn't always the easiest or least stressful time. He wasn't a great believer in baby steps or in easing someone into the lineup. If he thought you ready, you were supposed to be ready for anything. Later in life, his players—whatever their place in the world—could apply this encouragement to associates and friends and loved ones.

Rod was the embodiment of the idea of a time to work and a time to play. This disposition isn't as easy to pass along as is the proper way to conduct oneself on a ball field or in a hotel or in a position of authority. Some people just seem to understand when to be serious and when to let off steam. Rod was one of them. His clowning, his "hamminess," and his practical jokes never interfered with his work or detracted from his ultimate standing as a serious force in the world. What he was showing is that you can let your hair down—or wear a funny wig over it—without losing either authority or respect as long as you maintain discipline and concentration after the laughter subsides—laughter that at times brought tears to his eyes and a loss of breath. He did enjoy himself.

Even the earnest souls and darker temperaments that inevitably appeared on his roster benefitted from the wackiness and perhaps learned to tolerate it in others later in life and to appreciate its value in the human drama because they had witnessed it in one of the most successful people they would ever meet. You might not be funny yourself. You might not have a highly developed sense of humor. But you couldn't miss its function as an emotional counterpoint to stress.

Coaches are in the business of organizing, planning, and preparing. How well they perform these functions is reflected in team performance. Rod ran an efficient ship. Above all, he ran a purposeful ship. Everything in practice had a time and place and a point. The program was brisk. But it lacked a feeling of rush or haste. The rhythm was consistent. Rod called the beat. It had no dead spots. "As a team practices, so it will play." Practices were designed to instigate a sense of purpose, to illustrate the best use of space and time, and to foster a residual feeling of a task completed well. If a player got the point, he'd take that feeling to the next set of tasks.

Rod didn't run elaborate drills or conditioning routines. Tom House, a former major league pitcher and author of numerous books on baseball, thinks that coaches in Rod's day, especially early in his career, counted on young players being already in shape to play baseball. Before organized kids' baseball limited innings and pitches, college pitchers went nine innings on weekends and occasionally threw an inning or two in midweek games. They might pitch the first game of a doubleheader and relieve in the second game. You wouldn't find players in the weight room.

Conditioning was straightforward. You threw and you ran. You spent time in the whirlpool or on the rubbing table. By today's standards, it was all very basic. I'm not qualified to take a position on the relative strengths and weaknesses of older and new conditioning programs. I refer to Rod's unadorned methods of conditioning because they showed again that "basics work." If they're the right basics. Keep it simple and do it right. The concept looms large in his legacy.

Rod's "drills" were game situations. You worked on the bunt play, the relay play, the pickoff play, and the rundown play with suitable defensive alignments and shifts. At all times, Rod stressed execution of the fundamentals. As has been said, these drills were intended to install "good habits." Do it right now and you'll do it right in a game. Without having to think. Good habits work everywhere. You'll see when you're a lawyer.

Rod was a sophisticated man who dealt with thorny situations in all phases of life. He knew better than to give the impression that practice and preparation can guarantee a reflexively correct response to every crisis, even a mild one. Life is too complicated. Sometimes, you do have to think—and think hard. But he knew that if you have your feet under you—physically and psychologically—you have a solid foundation for the concerted mental energy required to navigate through life. You'll keep your composure and your wits about you. Or at least the chances are better that you will. We got it. We understood that we were "practicing" to confront events more important than the bunt play. However, make no mistake. At the moment, the bunt play was the most important event on Earth. You better believe it.

House says that "he looked forward to practice every day." He enjoyed the experience for itself, not only as a preparation for games. You were learning how to get things done in an atmosphere that was intended to reach beyond the confines of a ballpark. That sentiment is echoed by Pat Gillick, a Hall of Fame general manager, whose teams in Toronto (1992 and 1993) and Philadelphia (2008) won the World Series. Pat learned organization on the ball field and on trips, and in our conversation, he singled out Rod's accomplishments as an entrepreneur. He put into a few words what we all felt—day in and day out: "Rod was the kind of coach you wanted to play for." Both of these men say what I've heard over and over from his players. Rod taught by example. He was the kind of coach you not only wanted to play for but to also learn from.

All this constituted a lesson in how to appreciate and apply the virtue of design and order and how to keep track of the little things. You learned to exploit the confidence that comes with a feeling of readiness. It's hard to think of any productive activity in life where these virtues don't apply—whether or not one is officially in charge. It starts with being in charge of oneself. On this point, Rod was adamant. Although he came to California as a kid, he was raised in a New Orleans family at a time when the old Southern code of the gentleman was still operative. Enacted by Rod, it had no superfluous gestures or frills. He wanted us to learn to behave appropriately in all situations, and he put a high premium on keeping your composure. Although he never said it in so many words, as far as I know, his message was to show the world you can be counted on.

The legacy is the man himself. It's still hard to believe that he's gone. Years could pass, as they do, but in a phone conversation, he wouldn't skip a beat. He'd take you back to an event when you made him proud. Or he'd tease a little. Or he'd repeat an old story with new embellishments. He was resolved to preserve and, in an instant, to reclaim every memory that had enriched his own life. That heritage was renewed when he heard the voice of one of his tigers.

These phone chats took on a special significance after he retired from coaching. The subject could be almost anything or nothing in particular—the time brief. All that mattered was that the connection was being sustained. For him, it was a tonic. You could hear it—another note in his musical range.

Small encounters also occurred at an event, at a baseball game, or at halftime at a USC football game. He neither sought nor shunned the spotlight. People naturally gravitated to him. He attracted a crowd. He didn't always have much time to visit. But a few words or a gesture kept the connection alive. He made it his business to notice every tiger in the vicinity. These moments away from the ball field and away from publicity were special in their way. Maybe they weren't intimate moments—more like refueling ones. They're also strokes in the memorable picture of the man.

When Rod accepted the award as Coach of the Century, he said, "This doesn't mean much unless you can repeat." For his players, he's still repeating.

4

Images of a Legend

Rod with his sisters Leah and Grace

Rod with his dog and his bird, Polly

Rod as a player at Hollywood High School

1930 Rod and Babe Ruth article

Pickoff play by Rod and Ken Peters at USC

Rod as a player at USC

Rod as a player for the Brooklyn Dodgers

1935 Dayton Ducks

Rod strolling through the streets of LA

Rod and Helen's engagement photo

Rod in his early days as the USC baseball coach

Rod with Joe DiMaggio

1942 CIBA championship team (Rod's first championship team)

1948 NCAA championship team with batboy Sparky Anderson (USC's first national championship in baseball)

Rod with Tris Speaker

Rod with Casey Stengel in 1951 at the game between the New York Yankees and the Trojans on Bovard Field

Rod wearing the red wig with sons Terry and Justin

Rod with Casey Stengel wearing the red wig

Rod with his USC coach, Sam Barry

Rod with one of his six Coach of the Year awards

Rod and his son Justin with two of Rod's Coach of the Year trophies and his Japan USA Series trophy

Rod with Mickey Mantle, son Justin, and grandsons Marc and Brett

Rod with one of his DART trucks

Rod with his son Terry

1964 Tokyo Olympics coaching staff

1968 NCAA champions

Major League All-Stars putting the red wig on Rod

Rod hitting a fungo

1971 NCAA championship team

1972 NCAA championship team

1974 NCAA championship team

Rod with Bill "Spaceman" Lee

Rod with Steve Kemp, Roy Smalley, Fred Lynn, and Dave Kingman at an alumni game

Rod with Tom Seaver

Rod with former batboy Sparky Anderson

Rod at the 1984 Los Angeles Olympics

Rod on the set of *Field of Dreams*

Rod with President George Bush and Peter O'Malley

The Dedeaux family at Rod's retirement party in 1986

The Dedeaux family breaking ground for Dart's 875,000 square foot warehouse in Ontario, California

The Dedeaux family at Rod and Helen's 50th wedding anniversary party

Rod and Helen's 50th wedding anniversary party

The cast of *A League of Their Own* working out with Rod at Surfside

Rod with Geena Davis on the set of *A League of Their Own*

Rod with Joe DiMaggio and Tommy Lasorda

Rod with John Wooden

Rod and Helen

Rod being inducted into the USC Hall of Fame in 1994

Rod with son Justin and Tom Seaver at USC Hall of Fame ceremony in 1995

Rod being honored at a USC Homecoming

Rod with his daughter Denise at the 1996 Atlanta Olympics

Rod wearing his decoration from the emperor of Japan

Rod at the party in Tokyo after he was decorated by the emperor of Japan

Rod with Randy Johnson

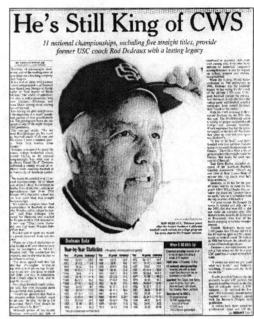

He's Still King of CWS

*11 national championships, including five straight titles, provide
former USC coach Rod Dedeaux with a lasting legacy*

1999 College World Series article

Rod with Sparky Anderson at Anderson's
induction into the Baseball Hall of Fame in
2000

Rod with Tommy Lasorda at the 2000
Sydney Olympics

Rod with Arnold Schwarzenegger

Rod with President George W. Bush

Rod with Mike Scioscia

Rod with (from left to right) Joe Morgan, Ann Meyers Drysdale, Bill Sharman, and Al Michaels

Rod with the USC marching band

Rod being honored for his five consecutive national championships

Rod and Helen

Rod with Vin Scully at Rod's 90th birthday party

Rod surrounded by friends and former players at his 90th birthday party

Memorial to Rod at the 2006 College World Series

Pallbearers at Rod's funeral

Rod's 2006 College World Series seat at Rosenblatt Stadium in Omaha, Nebraska

Rod's son Terry, great-granddaughter Kayla, granddaughter Galyn, and son Justin in front of Rod's photo at TD Ameritrade Park in Omaha, Nebraska

5

A Trojan Remembers the Master

I tried out for the USC freshman baseball team in 1950. I'd come from Providence, Rhode Island, and had appeared out of nowhere. Forrest Twogood, the coach, was amused by an uninvited boy at 5'7" and 145 pounds who aspired to pitch for the Trojans. But Twogie kept me on the team. He was in the habit of calling me "the little man" with a twinkle in his eye.

In 1951, after the death of Sam Barry, Rod Dedeaux became head baseball coach at the university. And there I was again. A lot of coaches might have humored me for a while and then dismissed me gently. I didn't throw hard, and I certainly didn't look like one of Rod's "tigers." But he wasn't a conventional judge of talent. Part of his genius was that he searched for something in a prospective player. If he found it, he nurtured it.

In my case, he saw a "little man" who wanted desperately to pitch for him, who took coaching, and who worked very hard. I had good control and, as he often said, "wasn't afraid." For a start, that was enough for Rod. Always ahead in his thinking, he looked down the road to fit me into his scheme. I was given a uniform.

He immediately gave me a trial to test my attitude. During batting practice, a pitcher is assigned to stand behind the mound with a brown bag of balls and to feed the man throwing batting practice. It's an important but humbling job. You're just a relay cog in the machine. Far more often than any other pitcher, I heard Rod yell, "Little Davie, big brown bag." ("Big Brown Bag" should have been listed as my position in the program.) I did my duty uncomplainingly, but Rod saw that I was tugging at the leash. One day, he took me for an amble up the first base line and into the outfield. I received my first "shave and haircut." That term referred to a pep talk in a soft voice while he was also massaging your shoulder. He said: "I know you want to pitch. If you didn't, I wouldn't have you out here. I know you think you can do better than some of the others. If you didn't, you wouldn't have a uniform. That's the point. You have to prepare yourself to do better. You have to be ready when your chance comes. It might come only once."

Rod pitched me in a few scattered innings in pre-season games, but I was still low on the chart. Then, Stanford came to town for the first league series. I was in the bullpen, not expecting to see action. In the seventh inning, our starter ran into trouble. Rod came to the end of the dugout, wiggled the sign for a pitcher to start warming up, and held his palm close to the ground. That meant me. Twogie, then the pitching coach, was pleased to see I was getting the call. He stood behind me, offering encouragement while I was warming up. Then, I heard him say, "He wants you, Davie." I handed my warm-up jacket to the senior manager on the way to the mound. For the first time, I was being summoned in the middle of an inning. The bases were loaded with one out. We trailed by one run.

Trojan fans were probably asking themselves and one another, "Who is this?" Rod handed me the ball. He looked me straight in the eye. He watched me throw strikes during warm-up. Then, he said: "Keep the ball down and we'll get two. Then, we'll win this one for you." These words were spoken as if they were already a statement of fact. I believed.

On the second pitch, the batter hit a nice two-hop ball to our shortstop. We "got two." The inning was over. I thought the man was a wizard. He chose the right situation to give me that "one chance." He risked the game. But he played favorable odds. He needed a low-ball pitcher who didn't issue walks. He won the bet, and we won the game. I saw him make that sort of move regularly during my three years on the varsity and later as his assistant.

Lesson number one. Prepare. Prepare. Prepare. Keep your head in the game even when you're not playing. Maintain the right attitude. Be patient. Be ready. That lesson isn't limited to the baseball field.

My close friend Hal Charnofsky learned the same lesson. He was the shortstop half of a double-play combination with his twin brother Stan. But in 1951, for the second year in a row, Hal was playing behind Bobby Lillis, the best shortstop in college baseball. It was hard on Hal because Stan was in the starting lineup. Then, one of our outfielders suffered a freak injury. Instead of filling the vacancy with a reserve outfielder, Rod called on Hal. It might have seemed like another surprising choice. Not when you consider that Hal was an excellent hitter and bunter and a smart base runner, and he didn't make mistakes. He played a major role in our winning the league championship. It was poetic justice that I was on the mound and he caught the last out in the game against UCLA that clinched the pennant. Two boys who began the season on the bench vindicated Rod's decision to give them that "one chance."

After the Stanford game, for the remainder of the league season, Rod brought me into several games in tight situations. He soon had me believing, as he said each time, that "this is just the way you like it, Davie." Indirectly, he was illustrating a larger theme:

Train a person to do a job, keep giving him that job, and convince him he's the best man for the job. Confidence will be repaid.

I might have been prepared to be the "fireman," but nothing could have prepared me for what happened in the final playoff game for the Pacific Coast Conference championship and a trip to the College World Series. We won the first game of the series but were blown out in the second game by Oregon State. The Beavers came equipped with big lumber from Corvallis. When the game was out of hand, Rod sent Tom Kemp, a starter, and me to the locker room. There, minus uniform tops, Tom and I discussed the opposing hitters as if he'd soon be facing them.

In the locker room between games, the mood was upbeat, even after a crushing defeat. We had sodas, oranges, and chocolate bars. Like kids at a picnic. The hum of voices was steady.

Rod wouldn't tolerate defeatism. His attitude always was "We'll get 'em next time." Next time was 20 minutes ahead. I was sitting on a rubbing table, legs dangling, and talking to a teammate. Suddenly, Rod appeared. He extended a baseball toward me. I must have looked stunned. He said, "You want it, don't you?" I couldn't speak, but I took the ball. He said nothing more. No pep talk. He asked if I wanted the ball. I took it. That was that. He went to talk to another player.

He was choosing to start the game on which the season hung with a sophomore who hadn't started a game all year.

Twogie and I went upstairs and across the diamond to the bullpen. He said, "There's plenty of time." I didn't hurry. I wasn't nervous. Maybe I didn't have time to become nervous.

We scored three runs in the first inning. But in the second inning, the bats that had pulverized us in the first game exploded on me. Four runs were in. Runners were on first and third with one out. As Rod jogged to the mound, I sneaked a look at the bullpen. (Sneaked because he always said, "Don't look for help.") No one was throwing.

He said: "You're doing fine. Keep throwing strikes. We'll get two. This is your game." He didn't linger. He didn't elaborate.

The next batter hit into a double play and we were out of the inning. (The wizard again.) I ran out of gas with one on and one out in the ninth. The reliever threw one pitch and got another double play. We were on our way to Omaha.

Some of the Trojan fans must have been uneasy about Rod's decision to leave me in the game. But he was demonstrating his principle that you don't panic when the weather turns stormy. You bull your neck. With a few words, the tone of voice, and eye contact, he communicated his confidence to me and to my teammates. I think he was also sending to the other team the message that this little guy is going to hang in there and get you out. His visit to the mound served two purposes. The man was always one jump (at least) ahead.

My parents were in attendance that day, accompanied by a family friend from out of town who'd graduated from Oregon State oddly enough. Between games, my dad and Phil Welty, his sales manager, went to the small concession stand outside the park for hot dogs. They heard the thumping of the catcher's glove. The starter for the decisive game was warming up. My dad said, "I'll see how Tom [Kemp] looks." Tom was the obvious choice to start. He'd been starter number three all season long. My dad, hot dog in hand, made his way through the other watchers and disappeared from view. When he re-emerged, he said only "It's Dave." The hot dog bun was empty. He hadn't eaten it. He didn't notice he was carrying an empty bun back to his seat. Phil always maintained that the father of the surprise starter had to be guided back to his seat.

Dad had a long, anxious afternoon but survived until the happy ending—just barely, according to observers. That night, at a dinner party, he was seated at a table with a man with pudgy hands and flashy rings who talked nonstop about his coups in the real estate market. Dad was eager to talk only about the game. The most sympathetic ear, that of his cousin Bill, was seated two tables away. They did manage to grab a few minutes together in the kitchen. My mom said, "Your father had almost as much trouble getting through the evening as through the game."

I didn't see him until the next morning when I came out for breakfast. He was putting on his best imitation of a man who "knew we had it all the way." Finally, he had complete freedom to talk about the game. But he asked a few casual questions, commented on a few plays, and briefly congratulated his son. Normally a talkative and ebullient man, he was offhanded to the point of insouciance. But when it came time to take the dog for a walk and buy the Sunday paper, he had to return to the house to pick up the dog.

The baseball gods, always fickle, deserted Hal and me in Omaha. The winning runs in an elimination game were scored against me when Hal tried for a shoestring catch and the ball skipped past him to the fence. He and I were crestfallen. Rod concealed his own disappointment when he consoled us. First, he told the manager of the hotel to remove all razor blades from our rooms. Then, he said to Hal and me: "Hold your heads up, tigers. Without you, we would never have made it to Omaha."

You did your best. Men take defeat in stride. Another day will come. That's a lesson for life. Not least, he reminded us of past achievements.

The most important thing is to keep people believing in themselves.

Rod always said the right thing at the right time. One time, the right thing was out of character. In my senior year, as a starting pitcher, I failed to cover first base at UCLA on a ball hit to the right side of the infield. Rod greeted me in the dugout with "God dammit, Davie, you're out there because you don't make mistakes." I'd never heard him raise his voice to a player before that moment or swear on the field. (His strongest oath was "What in the world?") He made a tour of the dugout and returned to slip his arm around my shoulder. A shave and haircut was coming. I deserved the sting, but he didn't let it linger.

I never asked him, but I often wondered why I was the singular recipient of wrath expressed in public (as far as I know). One of my teammates had an explanation. "He couldn't believe what he just saw." Years later, another said: "Because you were one of his favorites. You let him down." The man had an awful lot of "favorites." No doubt I embarrassed him by betraying his trust that I would always make that play right. I made both of us look bad. But it wasn't just that play. A history was behind his feelings. I was his creation. It started with those long stints on the big brown bag. He selected an unlikely prospect. He nurtured me into the pitcher that served both of our interests. He continually praised my strengths—sometimes in front of the whole team. "See how Davie strides in from the bullpen. He wants the ball." Any self-satisfaction I might have felt was washed away on one occasion. In the showers, someone piped up: "Anyone got a ball. Davie wants the ball." Someone else said, "In the shower?" The original voice said: "Anywhere. He always wants the ball. Get him a ball."

Rod took my blunder at UCLA as a personal affront.

Rod's lessons stuck even when you didn't have the ball because he was, above all, a great teacher. He had an acute and nimble mind and the gift of precise speech. He used those endowments to instruct and to inspire. Great teachers are great psychologists. (As Stan expressed in Chapter 5.) Rod was one of the best. He knew when to put the pressure on and when to afford breathing room. A look (sometimes stern—the one his kids mentioned), a gesture, a tone, a funny crack, an anecdote, a smile, a wink, a massage, a few words, even the appearance of a man betrayed ("My God, I'm making him ill") were elements in his inventory. Everyone who knew him was aware of his social skills. He relied on them to time perfectly an interaction with a player or with the whole team. Each player was a project—in the best sense of that term. Rod aimed to make each project a success not only on the field but off the field—at the time and later in life.

Not only did I apply the mentality he taught to my coaching but also to my teaching as a professor of English and to performing administrative duties. Whenever I was tempted to slack off doing research or preparing a manuscript, I could almost hear him saying: "Details, tiger. Details." Play the game right off the field too. I can't claim that I always played the game right off the field, but I never forgot that I was supposed to.

Even after you graduated, Rod was always ready to help. In 1958, I coached a community college team in Coalinga, California. I called and asked if he could arrange for our school to purchase the professional model of Louisville Slugger bats. He did even better. He routed a DART truck through Coalinga in the middle of the night. The cargo of bats was transferred from the truck into a local police car. The cop had had a cup of coffee with a major league team. He said, "Your coach sure takes care of his men." He got that right.

That same year, he brought his Trojans to that little town off the beaten path to play my Falcons. It was a big event. And a heck of a game. The Trojans won 9 to 8, but our tying and winning runs were on their way to the plate in the bottom of the ninth when Freddie Scott, the USC shortstop, made a great play to end the game. Rod said, "We were lucky to get out of there alive."

After the game, I brought Rod to a party at our athletic director's house. All the other coaches at the college and the high school coaches in town were awed in the presence of the legend. But Rod quickly put them at ease with his charm and humor—some of it at my expense. One of them said to me the next day, "I see what you mean."

That year, his team won the NCAA national championship; mine, the California junior college championship. When I saw him in the summer, I thanked him for his training, the bats, the game in Coalinga. I reported that I'd said to a scout who liked the way the Coalinga team played, "I learned it all from the master." "Naw," Rod said. "You made me look good."

Over the years, if you called with a request, he'd say "I'll get right on it." And he did. They say that if you want something done, find a busy man. But not all busy men are as accommodating as was Rod.

No profile of this extraordinary man is complete without another example of his skullduggery, which I will put up there with the shrinking finger. The truth is that you couldn't turn your back on him for a minute. You weren't safe from the front either. After his varsity and my freshman team had played games against service teams in San Diego, he and I and his entourage went to see jai alai in Tijuana. Shortly, he said, "C'mon, Coach, let's get a beer." I thought he meant at a concession stand. But he hustled me out into the street and hailed a cab. "I know a great place," he said.

The place was a small cantina on a dingy back street. It was bright. Happy music was playing. We took a booth and compared notes on the games that day. He seemed very earnest as he fielded questions about strategy. (You never missed a chance to pick his brain.) Then, he excused himself to go to the restroom. When he returned, we resumed the shop talk. Suddenly, I was aware that a voluptuous woman had slid into the booth and sidled up to me. She smiled, pulled me to her, and said something about "amor." Rod said: "Go ahead, Coach. Have a good time. Mum's the word. If you miss the bus, take a cab back to the base. I'll pay the tab."

I was trying to disentangle myself from arms and bosoms. The woman was strong.

Rod kept saying, "He's very good." Then, stickler for details in all situations, he said, "Don't forget your jacket afterward."

The woman's eyes lit up. She repeated "Very good." And broke into a broader smile. And held me tighter.

The rascal. The woman was the niece of Joe Gonzalez, Rod's former teammate at USC. He'd set the whole thing up on his trip to the "restroom." In fact, he'd probably planned the prank before we crossed the border. Silly me, I thought he'd vacated the jai alai games mainly to escape the hangers-on. The great man wanted my company only. Mine—and that of a good-natured fellow conspirator named Rosa.

Rod's alumni include professors and teachers, school administrators, coaches, dentists and doctors, architects, lawyers and businessmen, pharmacists, and engineers. He remembered every one of us and could astonish you by bringing up a game—even a specific play—in which you were involved. His uncanny memory stretched back more than a half century.

We were all influenced by him. We're all indebted to him. We have all applied his lessons to life outside of baseball. To his last day, we were still his "tigers."

On a very big day, players on his teams from the 1940s onward stood behind Rod on Dedeaux Field to honor him on his 90th birthday. Accolades came from Vin Scully and Tommy Lasorda, among others. But I'd bet it was the presence of all those tigers that moved him most. He wiped moisture from his eyes.

Very few people can claim with justice that they're the best ever in their field. Rod Dedeaux was one of them. But he never made the claim for himself—or would. He didn't have to. Everyone else did it for him.

My daughter was present at the USC game where I last saw Rod. A batter hit a weak pop-up that fell in foul territory about halfway to third base. Rod said, "That's about as far as your dad could hit 'em."

Wonderful. Right to the end.

6

Rod Dedeaux:
Baseball Psychologist

Stan Charnofsky
Second Baseman

At a USC Trojan Club celebration in the San Fernando Valley, Hall of Fame manager Sparky Anderson said: "This Dedeaux man is not only the *college* coach of the century. He is the *coach of the century*—period."

I had the privilege of playing for Rod for four years, then coaching for him for a couple more. What boggles the mind—along with his 11 national titles—is how he was able to be concerned and be aware about the personal growth and development of every one of his players. Some years ago, at a Trojan baseball game, he was explaining to friends seated around him about my twin brother, Hal, and me—shortstop and second base way back in the early 1950s—how we had doctorates and headed up our departments at our prospective universities. *That* was what made him proud. Another of his former players, seated nearby, Dave Rankin, a relief pitcher specialist also from the 1950s, Rod lauded for receiving his doctorate at the University of London and being an English professor at a state university.

Rod wove tale after tale about his players who had become successes in life. One wonders if all those well-lived lives were a coincidence or if Rod's mentor status had something to do with them. Let me count the ways:

"You *never* drop a throw," Rod would tell me. "It is a mental mistake. You can't control a bouncing ball, so physical errors will occur, but games are won or lost on mental errors." In the dugout was a fine pad: 10 cents for each mental mistake, and at the end of the season, a party paid for by those who trespassed most.

"You *never* make a bad throw. If you set your feet, you throw straight." Rod was a "puppies" man. "Move those puppies," he'd call out. Because I was a second base man, moving my feet quickly and skillfully meant avoiding getting spiked or bowled over by sliding base runners. He'd admonish my twin brother to feed me perfectly every time. "Stan can't handle the ball well and get it to first base in time if you don't throw it to his glove." And then, to me he'd say: "You have to get there early. You have to be on balance. You can't expect the ball to be thrown perfectly to you every time, but you *still* have to handle it and get rid of it to first base." Each and every player had to do his job the *right* way. "One set of rules" was Rod's motto.

"You will be the best pivot man on the double play in *the world,*" Rod would tell me, over and over, until I believed him. Now, as a psychologist, I recognize that he, Rod, was the master psychologist. Maybe that's what coaching is all about—his magnificent secret—the psychology of building and never tearing down.

In my sophomore year, Rod would fungo balls to my left, time after time, just out of my reach,—sometimes for 15 minutes straight—and then say to me: "If you run that ball down, it's an out. From the grass in right field, it's a short throw to first base or even to second. No ball can get by you." I'd go into the locker room after practice, irritated by my failure and frustrated at Rod's insistence. By the time I was a senior, I understood what he meant. I recall chasing a ball to my left in a critical game situation, spearing it with my glove, spinning with my back to home plate, and firing to second base, where Hal relayed it to first for a double play. Rod's belief in me became my belief in myself.

Rod jokingly called my brother and me "sandblowers"—his way of announcing we were little and built close to the ground. Considering our small stature, we weren't power hitters, although occasionally, we would jack one out of the park. I led the conference once in triples because I could run. Hal led the conference in hitting his senior year. He was first-team All-American shortstop (that year, three shortstops were selected and no second or third basemen; the three were Hal, Dick Groat, and Harvey Kuenn). Rod never forgot the honors his players receive and could rattle them off as if they were plays in the playbook or written out on his sleeve. At 90-plus, he had a keen memory for games, statistics, players, and achievements, going back to the first great team in 1948.

Rod called my brother and me into his office just before the season began in our senior year. "You two no longer need to worry about your output," he said. "You are on top of your games, and I am asking you to be my co-captains so you can help out with your teammates." In other words, he was communicating to us that we weren't problems to ourselves so we could focus on problems outside of ourselves.

My physical talent was okay, although not major league caliber. But Rod knew how to pull from me (and just about everyone else) the best possible effort. For one, he'd call me "Pepper," alluding to my hustle and energy. "You never walk on the ball field," he'd say. "If you get a base on balls, run to first. When the inning is over, run off the field. When the catcher throws the ball back to the pitcher with a man on third, move over a couple of steps to back it up—you must always anticipate it might be thrown badly." As a model, he'd trot out to the mound to visit a pitcher.

He kept us loose. We always had the "red wig" caper—where sophomores would be made to wear a Mortimer Snerd–type red wig in airports and buses. People would stare, the rest of us would break up, and the sophomore would be initiated. No wonder we didn't go onto the field scared or uncertain. We expected to do well. We played for each other. We were winners.

After games, when we won, we would sing "McNamara's Band"—all of us—in the locker room while Rod moseyed about, touching us, smiling, giving us light massages on our shoulders and necks. Some of us applied the label "a shave and a haircut" whenever Rod wanted to speak to a player privately. "Oh, oh, be ready for the shave and the haircut." He never admonished a player—I don't believe I *ever* saw him do it—in front of other players. Corrections were always learning moments—always private—and, in the end, appreciated as aids to our baseball acumen.

The logic of Rod's tactics may not have been fully appreciated by us when we played for him. He always had the starting nine sit next to each other on the bench when we were at bat and the pitcher and catcher would be told to sit side by side. His reasoning? "If you are right next to each other and a thought comes up about a pitch, a play, the other team's strengths, some strategy we want to employ, you'll say it out loud. If someone is 20 feet down the bench, you may think it but not bother to say it." Communication was always the medium and teamwork the end goal.

These days, when you see a third base coach or manager go through a dozen movements, touching his cap and face and arm and shirt, you wonder at the unnecessary complication of it all. Rod was a master of simplicity. If he wanted to give you a "hit" sign, he'd put his hand out flat just below his belt and call out "Make it be a good pitch." Did he care if the other team knew you were hitting, not taking? Sure, but not as much as he cared about you, the hitter, feeling empowered by his encouragement.

Discovering Rod's strategic approach might lead one to think he was cerebral about baseball—only in his head—or perhaps not aggressive enough. It wasn't true. He'd say to us, "Tigers, this game of baseball has no time limit, like football or basketball. You could be ahead by 10 runs and the other team could rise up and overtake you in the ninth inning. So, when you get ahead, you don't relax with the lead—you step on 'em harder. If you have five runs, get five more. If you have 10, get 10 more. Don't give 'em any idea they can come back and beat you."

Rod believed in the right way and the wrong way. Sometimes, you did things the right way and they didn't work out. That never swayed him. It was the correct baseball move. It was the percentage play. Once in Omaha, at the College World Series, Bobby Lillis, who went on to play and coach for many years in the big leagues, was thrown out stealing in the ninth inning and Tennessee beat the Trojans by a run. Rod's reaction? "It was the right thing to do. We needed him in scoring position. He'd make that steal eight out of 10 times. It's just the breaks of the game."

His friendship with Casey Stengel brought the New York Yankees to Bovard Field (now rebuilt and named Dedeaux Field) for a spring exhibition game back in 1951. The grandstands were bulging and the cheers deafening, and we played with our hearts in our throats against Joe DiMaggio, Phil Rizutto, Johnny Mize, Vic Raschi, Hank Bauer, Jerry Coleman, and a young rookie named Mickey Mantle. The Trojans lost 15 to 1, but each team had two double plays, each team made an error, and the difference was the Yankees getting 20 hits and the Trojans five. As for Mantle, he had two homers, a triple, and a single, and the one time we got him out, he smashed a one-hop liner to second base that almost knocked me into right field—but we threw him out at first. Rod used that game to build our confidence as a team. "The only college team the Yankees played," "We can hold our heads up high," "We played good mental baseball," "Don't forget—they are big leaguers, and even more, they are the Yankees."

Bill Sharman is known as an All-American and all-pro basketball player who later coached in the NBA. He was also a gifted baseball player, with fluid actions, a fine arm, and good power at the plate. In his senior year at USC, in the middle of the season, he hit two grand slam home runs against Santa Clara University, and after the game, he was offered a bonus contract with the Brooklyn Dodgers. Bill was already married and needed the money, so he told Rod he'd likely take the offer. Rod's reaction was to congratulate him, but he also asked him to come to a team meeting to explain to his teammates his rationale. It was a brilliant move because it communicated to us that Bill wasn't deserting us willy-nilly, and it also broadcast loud and clear that when our performances reached a similar level, we would also have a shot at pro ball. Instead of a betrayal, we looked at Sharman's choice as an inspiration.

Of course, one is admired when he wins, but with Rod, he did it whether a player had big league talent or not. It was the chemistry he was able to create that made his teams jell. Yes, he coached Mark McGwire and Tom Seaver and Fred Lynn and Randy Johnson and 50 other big leaguers. But he also coached those of us who never got to the "show," and he made *men* of us.

At one of the parties for his 90th birthday celebration, Rod went around the room and told anecdotes about everyone in attendance—some 40 people. His memory for people and baseball events stuns the senses. How does one explain that skill? Perhaps it's best to simply label it "genius" and let it go at that.

On Dedeaux Field, at the grand celebration of his 90th, 60 of his former players were asked to come out onto the field and be honored, after which his family was invited out. His children and many grandchildren surrounded him, and he said to the crowd, "When you see my family, you realize I didn't spend all my time on the ball field."

I usually batted second in our lineup, and Rod kept stressing the importance of hitting behind the runner—to the right field side. I worked hard on the skill, and it served me well during my four college years and several more in the minor leagues. I rarely hit into a double play. Today, the skill seems to be a lost art. Players swing from their heels—the home run their *only* goal—and grounding into double plays isn't even thought about twice. Ah, well, we'll get them next time. With Rod, you played as if there wouldn't be a next time.

In all, this Dedeaux fellow is a baseball legend. When one was near him, an aura permeated the vicinity. He's the epitome of charisma. He attracts everyone around him: former players, fans, children, baseball people, Trojans from other sports. Once, at a home baseball game, Anthony Davis, who scored five touchdowns against Notre Dame in one half, sought Rod out for a few minutes of conversation. A little boy of about nine or 10 asked Rod to sign his baseball bat. A fan seated nearby said he was going to the concession stand and would Rod like a hot dog and soda. At Los Angeles Coliseum football games, he'd often bring Casey Stengel as his guest, and in later years, it was Tommy Lasorda.

I began this treatise noting how Rod was not only concerned about his players' on-the-field performances but also their outside lives. Could his mentoring have been influential in so many of us living successful professional lives? A psychologist helps folks clarify their life dilemmas. A baseball psychologist builds character that goes beyond the ball field. Perhaps it's clearer now why I consider Rod a *master* psychologist. Without him seeming to think about it, his every comment and every action were designed to promote self-confidence in his players. That self-confidence became hallmarks for us in the greater game of life. I can't tell you how many times I have said to my students: "Do you realize how talented you are? You can reach for anything you choose. You are a one-of-a-kind marvel." I have no doubt in my mind where I learned that philosophy. A final example will close out this essay and hopefully illustrate my transcendent respect for this remarkable human being.

In my senior season, we were playing at Oregon for the Pacific Coast title and the chance to go to the College World Series. It was down to the last out of the game, and we had men on base when I came to bat. After a couple of pitches, I hit a ball as hard and as deep as any in my baseball career. The field has no fence in center, and the Oregon player ran down my drive and caught it some 400 feet away. I was devastated and depressed. While Rod was deeply disappointed, his consistent and upbeat style turned even that terrible loss into a teachable moment. "Pepper," he told me, "you'll never hit a ball better than that. In any other stadium, it's out of the park and we win. It's not the end. You'll see. It's the beginning for you."

He was right. Roy Hamey, head Yankee scout, was at the game. A few weeks later, I signed a bonus contract with the Yankees and started my professional career. It was successful, although it didn't take me to the big league club, and applying Rod's outlook, I was able to say: "Look what I did. Now it's time to switch gears and find another direction for my talents."

Rod Dedeaux, coach of the century, teacher deluxe, mentor sublime, an example to everyone, a man for all (baseball and other) seasons. He was *the* prototype baseball manager. He was *the* master psychologist. He *is* a full-fledged member of the Hall of Fame of Life.

7

Personal Tributes and Memories

Bob Burns
(Pitcher)

As we all know, Rod had the gift of gab. I can remember two specific instances where a simple "No" would have answered the question, but number one went farther and actually told us *why* he was saying no. Although sometimes farfetched, when he got done, we really did not have a comeback for it.

Example 1: We have all heard the words "Tiger … got to get a chop-chop" when the hair was a little long. When asked why we needed to get a haircut, I remember Rod replying, "Tiger, there is no reason to have your hair long, except to keep your head warm, and that is why we have hats." How do you argue with that?

Example 2: The guys would always complain that we needed pockets in our practice pants (for tobacco, etc.). I remember when the issue was brought to Rod, instead of just saying "No," his reply was: "Tiger, there is a reason that we do not have pockets in the practice pants. If we had pockets in the pants, then instead of putting a ball in the bucket when you were done with it, you would put it in your pocket. At the end of practice, you would forget that it was there, go home, and the ball would still be in your pocket, and before you know it, you would be in San Quentin." He was insinuating that he was saving us from starting a life of crime that started with stealing a baseball. Little farfetched, but how do you argue with that?

On another note, there is a story that I remember that is typical of number one. We all know he had the gift of gab, and whether he remembered who you were or not, he always made you feel like he knew exactly who you were and made you feel welcome. In one of our alumni games (which we had every year against all of the major leaguers that had played at USC), I had the opportunity to pitch two innings. I struck out a couple of these major leaguers (they were just starting to come out for spring practice and were obviously a bit rusty) and then I got to pitch to Dave Kingman. I was feeling pretty good after striking a couple out and delivered a fastball (fast for me was 65 mph). I can remember Dave "swatting" this ball like it was a nuisance to him—no effort at all. I have *never* seen a ball hit so hard or so far I my life. It was a line drive that was still going up as it went over the wall in left center at Dedeaux Field, and I never did see it start coming down. The USC-UCLA track meet was the next day at Drake Stadium at UCLA, and I always joked about how they probably started the 50-yard dash the next day when that ball finally hit the ground.

A few years later, I was working for Western Airlines and had a roommate that had grown up in Glendale and was very familiar with the name Rod Dedeaux. I had told him the story about this day I pitched to Dave Kingman. My roommate was a ticket agent for the airline and happened to check in first at the counter as the team was going to Honolulu for a tournament. He said, "Hey, aren't you the coach from USC?" He replied "Yes." My roommate said: "My roommate used to play for you. His name was Bob Burns." Rod replied, "Oh, yeah, good little ball player." My roommate continued: "Bob told me about a ball that Dave Kingman hit off him one day. Bob said that it just seemed to go forever, and he never did see it come down." Rod, never at a loss for words, replied, "Yeah, as I remember, he had quite a few like that."

Steve Busby
(Pitcher)

I was a cocky kid coming out of high school. But I was quickly taught lesson number one by Rod. You don't just show up and expect to play at USC—no matter how good you and others think you are. You can't be only as good as the competition to win a spot. You have to be better. You don't beat out or replace someone who is your equal. That lesson sank in and has remained with me for the remainder of my life. You work hard to become the best. It has served me well, and I've passed it along to people I've coached and taught.

It's a simple but consequential idea, like most of Rod's. Like his definition of the goal of pitching: "Hold 'em while we score two runs. Then, if you want to give up one run, you can. But you don't have to." You pitch to stay ahead until the game is won. I kept that in mind too as a big league pitcher, and I've taught it to young pitchers. Like all of Rod's players, I can think of many lessons about baseball and life that Rod taught. But these two come immediately to mind when I think back to my experience at USC from 1968 to 1971.

Jim Campanis
(Catcher/Infielder)

We didn't know it at the time, but my recruiting class would be Coach Dedeaux's last. That year we were invited to play a post-season tournament in Hawaii. As a freshman, I was excited to be sent in to pinch hit in the ninth inning of the last game and promptly smoked a one-hopper to the shortstop for a routine 6-4-3 double play. As it turned out, I was the last out in his legendary career. I feel fortunate to have played for Coach and will always remember his charisma, energy, and spirit.

Tim Coffin
(Pitcher)

Spring of 1970, I am a freshman pitcher. We are playing an intrasquad game. Another freshman and great friend, Bill Lazzarini (Lazz), a young phenom left-hander, is pitching to Dave Kingman. A group of pitchers are standing near Rod with Nate, our manager.

Lazz delivers his first pitch and the result was … iconic. To give the reader perspective, go back to the ball Albert Pujols of the St. Louis Cardinals hit off Brad Lidge of the Houston Astros in Game 5 of the 2005 NLCS. You remember that home run—the one that woke the NORAD computers in Cheyenne Mountain, sending them to Def-Con 4. The blast almost knocked the train off the tracks perched above left field at Minute Maid Park in Houston. Compared to the ball Kingman hit off Lazz that warm spring day, Pujols got jammed.

Rod watched the ball disappear over Bovard's left field fence, still rising fast, and commented "They may find that in Bakersfield." All of us, including Lazz, could hear this comment.

Lazz got the final out and slowly walked Rod's way and said, "Coach, I thought I could sneak a hanging curve by him." Rod looked at Lazz and then turned to Nate, saying "I'm dealing with freshman left-handers today. Call the 901 and order a bucket of suds. I'm going to need it." Lazz heard this too.

Lazz, being a bright guy, never forgot Rod's comments, putting the key words together: baseball, Bakersfield, and beer. A match made in heaven. Lazz graduated, his family bought the Budweiser distributorship in Bakersfield, and he has been fabulously successful with a wonderful life and family. Rod at his best.

Terry Dedeaux
(Second Baseman)

I have often been asked how my father became such a successful coach of a major baseball program as well as run a successful business. His schedule during the season was to be in the office at 6 a.m. until 2 p.m., when he would leave, go to USC for either practice or a game, then often be busy in the evening entertaining customers, attending business meetings, or a speaking at a USC event. Most thought that he just didn't sleep, but in fact, as he says, he was able to "sleep fast." He was able to sleep anywhere at any time for a quick cat nap to recharge his batteries.

Rod Dedeaux ran his business as he did his baseball team: as a dictator, master teacher, and great motivator. His focus for our organization was to pay great attention to detail, avoid mistakes by learning from others, measure our performance, and, of course, work hard at our jobs. As in sports, business is a competitive game, and he emphasized that we need to be prepared and on our toes at all times.

The DART organization, being a family business, was run in a family atmosphere. He took a special interest in everyone and their family and often would engage in group functions. He stressed the importance of teamwork to focus on our ultimate goals. It was the DART/Dedeaux family.

He also had the philosophy of establishing a long-term commitment to our customers, who he considered partners in our business with a common goal of providing superior service at a very competitive cost. It was stressed that it was most important that we understand their business and offer our suggestions for improvements, even if it was not to the benefit of our company.

That philosophy has played out with our partners, as many of them have been with Dart for over 50 years. Last but not least, he taught us to have fun and celebrate when there was success.

Tery Finigan
(Catcher)

Since I was associated with Rod over many years as a player, coach, employee of DART, and a friend, one story would be very difficult to choose. What I chose to write about is his approach to being a very successful coach and person.

When I became his assistant varsity coach in 1958—in those years, there was only one—he told me that the format for winning in college sports is to develop sound fundamentals and mental discipline at practice and then let the players play the game.

As you know, Rod was very organized, so each day prior to practice, we would chart the things we wanted to accomplish. We then put a time schedule together for each and posted it so that there wasn't any lost time. Many days, especially early in the year, we would repeat the fundamentals so they were totally understood. This meant that if the situation occurred in a game, it was not necessary for the player or players to spend time thinking about how to perform.

The mental discipline part of the equation was achieved on a daily bases in many ways, such as the use of the list of mental errors he would post during each game. The posting of each error meant that he did not have to address the error during the game, and not only did the player see the error, but all of the players could see it. The posting also meant he could maintain his philosophy of not coaching during the game because it might distract the player.

Rod had another philosophy that was a part of developing the mental side of the game and the person. He felt that a person had to be prepared or open to learning before you could teach. To achieve this, when there was a very important or personal issue, he would develop small steps or a special occurrence to make sure the player was open to his thoughts. Yes, sometimes a hand on the shoulder.

Orrin Freeman
(Pitcher)

I was fortunate enough to play and coach with Rod from 1968 through 1973. During those six years, we won five national championships. As I enter my 42nd year of working in baseball, I can hardly express how grateful I am for what I learned from Rod and Justin. Their teachings were the basis of our two World Series championships with the [Florida] Marlins.

Bob Hogue
(Pitcher)

I played baseball at USC from 1971–1973 (and graduated in 1975). I was a tall, lanky, seldom-used pitcher whose best attributes were retrieving foul balls that flew out of the park and/or keeping the pitching chart. As many young players knew, Coach Dedeaux called all of us "tiger." We suspected it was because he couldn't possibly remember our names. Because I hardly ever played, I was thoroughly convinced of that fact in my own case. I was proven totally wrong at the end of my freshman year, when I was working my summer job as an usher at Dodger Stadium.

My USC roommate, a nonathlete by the name of Russ Bledsoe who had never attended a USC baseball game or come anywhere near the practice diamond, was lucky enough to work the field level section when the USA baseball team came into the park, including Coach Dedeaux. Russ was thrilled to be able to seat the coach and several of the players and mentioned to Dedeaux that he was a USC student. Coach Rod took one look at my roommate's name tag and said: "Bledsoe, huh? You're Hogue's roommate." The coach then slapped Russ on the back and sat down.

When Russ told me that story, I was stunned—and also grinning ear to ear. Coach Rod Dedeaux did in fact know my name. Not only that, but he even knew my roommate's name. I was very proud to be called "tiger" from that day forward.

Tom House
(Pitcher)

I played for Rod Dedeaux. I am both proud and blessed to be able to say that. He was a difference maker who challenged me to go for it every day; to never settle; to do the right thing no matter what, on and off the field.

In the scheme of Trojan baseball, I fit somewhere between the bench jockey "Double Xers" and the future Hall of Famers who actually received degrees. In the scheme of professional baseball, I was an average major league pitcher and an innovative pitching coach. In the scheme of life, I am trying to follow in Rod's footsteps as a mentor and researcher for young people.

Rod was the college baseball Coach of the Century and a lot of things to many people. Most importantly, he was uniquely the same to each of us as individuals.

Jay Jaffe
(Outfielder)

I remember:

- 1968: We're playing Los Angeles State (now Cal State University at Los Angeles) for the District 8 championship and the right to go back to Omaha. We are down 4-1 in the ninth with two outs and two strikes on our batter. A base hit, a walk, another hit, and it is now 4-3. L.A. State had already packed their equipment, but they forgot that the fat lady had not sung yet. Ron Drake, as great a third baseman as there ever was, crossed home plate with the third run. Yours truly came to bat with the season on the line. As I am approaching the plate, Drake comes up to me and says, "Jay, if you don't get a hit, I'll kill you." I hit a big bouncer over the mound, over second base (just like the Dodgers in 1959). I get to first base as the ball arrives. I crash into the first baseman—the General, Jerry Feldman—and all I hear is Justin Dedeaux screaming at the top of his lungs. The ball miraculously fell out of Feldman's glove and we tied the score. We won it in the next inning. After the game, a reporter asked Rod: "So, Coach, you're down 4-1 in the ninth, two outs, and two strikes on your guy. What were you thinking?" Without skipping a beat, Rod replied, "Some people (emphasizing others but not Rod) thought we were in trouble."
- 1969: It's a Friday in April during spring break. We play UCLA for the championship of the Riverside National Collegiate Tournament on Saturday. UCLA coach Art Reichele has a three-hour practice scheduled for the Bruins. Rod and Art are staying at the Holiday Inn. Rod tells Brent Strom, Jim Barr, Randy Port, and me to check in with him in the dining room, where he will be having breakfast with Reichele that

Friday. At 8 a.m., the four of us walk into the dining room, and sure enough, Rod is sitting with Reichele having breakfast. Rod wishes us well. The four of us had just walked in with our golf clubs on our shoulders. No practice. Day off. The look on Reichele's face was priceless. We scored five runs in the first inning on our way to an 11-3 victory and the championship on Saturday.

Randy Johnson
(Pitcher)

I was a tall skinny kid who threw hard when I came to USC from the small town of Livermore, California. I was very raw. Rod gave me the opportunity to sink or swim at the college level. He always understood where his players were coming from. He was very patient. I became a starter in 1983 as a sophomore and continued in that role the next two years.

But my debut at USC was as a reliever. Rod called me into a game against Stanford on the road. I was very nervous. He said, "Are you ready?" I said, "Yes, I'll pitch from the stretch." He said, "Why? There's no one on base." I had mistaken the first base coach for a runner. I think it worked out.

Steve Kemp
(Outfielder)

Rod was always positive, and his leadership and positive attitude filtered down to us, his players. So, we never, ever doubted ourselves and knew that no one could beat us. We knew if we were down in the seventh inning that we were going to win. I know that other teams knew that as well because guys would say to me years later that they would be just waiting for something to happen that would end up in a loss for them.

Another thought was we were playing in Omaha against Texas and winning the game by a few runs, but it started to rain and it was only in the fourth or fifth inning. Rod wanted us to speed up the game so we would not get rained out, as we needed to get five full innings in to be a complete game. So, I hit a ball off the center field wall and could have had an easy triple but just jogged into third to get thrown out at third on purpose and when I got back to the dugout, he just looked at me like, "What were you doing?" We did win the game, however, and go on to win another national championship.

I would also say that Rod was like a father to me, and after not being drafted out of high school, he brought me into the program and, after my years at USC, made sure people knew who I was and that I was going to be able to further my career.

Marcel Lachemann
(Pitcher)

There are lots of very vivid images left from Rod that are very important time in my career in baseball. I am now closing in on 50 years of professional baseball, which include playing (Oakland Athletics) , coaching (Los Angeles Angels, Florida Marlins, USC, Colorado Rockies) , managing (Angels) and front office (special assistant to the general manager: Colorado and Angels). None of this could have been accomplished without the time spent playing and coaching for Rod.

Between Bob Lillis and myself, we are the only Trojan players fortunate enough to manage in the Major League. Rod was always an underlying influence. The number of things learned under Rod are very hard to single out, but if I had to pick one, it would be the "Never say die" mentality that he instilled in all of us. We were *never* out of a game and thus produced some of the all-time come-from-behind victories ever seen.

Using that as a theme for myself and trying to instill it on players has been a godsend for me. Rod was the greatest. They will never match his 11 national championship nor the influence he had on college baseball.

Vic Lapiner
(Pitcher)

Rod Dedeaux was a very important factor in my life. Baseball-wise, he taught us how to win, and he also taught us how to lose with grace and class.

Years ago I was inducted into the Southern California Jewish Sports Hall of Fame. In my speech that night, what I said about Rod was, he never saw religion, race, or color. All he cared about was could you play baseball and would you represent USC the right way.

In 1955, Rod took a team to the Far East. We played 27 games in 30 days, and our record was 24-3. My personal record on that trip was 9-0. That team put USC baseball on the international map. That trip, I also feel, was my personal legacy at USC.

It was and is still great to be a Trojan, and it was an honor to have played for Rod.

Fred Lynn
(Outfielder)

I learned more about how to play the game of baseball from Rod than any other coach or manager in my entire career. I am quite sure that this is not an unusual statement coming from anyone who ever played for Rod. On a more personal note, Rod would never let anyone try to coach or change the way I swung the bat. He liked what he saw and wasn't going to mess with it. But it wasn't a lock that I was going to be a center fielder and not a pitcher. I pitched my entire career at that point, including some time with the Pasadena Yankees, a semipro team. So, it was not until my sophomore year that it was finally decided. We were going to play a midweek game versus Loyola, a small school, but they had a very good hitting team.

I got to the field, and Coach told me that I was pitching. Normally, I would have been very excited to be on the hill, but I had a slight problem. I had played in a pickup basketball the night before and hyperextended my left arm. I couldn't tell Coach because we weren't supposed to be playing basketball. I warmed up and had nothing. I couldn't raise my arm to throw a curveball and had absolutely no fastball. Went out in the first inning, and I think I surprised the other team with the junk I was throwing up there and actually got three outs. They adjusted rather quickly and put up a four and five spot on me in the next two innings. Nine earnies in three frames. Coach never said much to me about that but never asked me to pitch again, thus sealing the deal that I would be a center fielder. I didn't tell coach about that until after my pro career was finished and we were at a USC baseball golf event, and he said, "Tiger, what time is it?" followed by the traditional shake of the head. "I knew something was wrong with you that day because you had the best fastball on the team, and that day, I could have caught you barehanded."

We had a good laugh about it, but it took me 20 years to tell him. I took that opportunity to tell Coach how much he meant to me and how his teachings helped me to be able to do the things that I did as a rookie and throughout my career. He made us all better players, but equally important to him was that we be good men as well.

Coach, we all miss you, and I hope I made you proud.

Art Mazmanian
(Second Baseman)

I introduced Rod as the speaker at Dorsey High School during my senior year. After graduation, I was headed to Los Angeles City College. My family could not afford to send me to a university.

Two weeks after the banquet, Rod called and offered me a baseball scholarship to USC. I was 5'5" and weighed 119 pounds. Rod had never seen me play. He made the offer on the basis of recommendations from Bud Brubaker, my coach at Dorsey, and from the principal.

I was stunned and delighted. That offer was the last thing I expected. I was thinking that because of my size, I wouldn't even make the team at LACC. One minute, I was worried about being cut from a junior college team; the next, I was hearing from the man himself that USC wanted me.

I was still only 17 when I entered the university. My classmates were mostly girls and men in uniform. Because of travel restrictions during the war, the Trojans played local teams, like Occidental, Cal Tech, Pepperdine, and UCLA. We had a mediocre season.

After a year in the Army, I returned to school in 1947 and joined a strong team that missed going to the College World Series by one game. Sam Barry, who had returned from the Navy, favored big players. But Rod always liked little guys if they had sufficient talent, brains, and courage. He worked me into enough games to qualify for a letter. (I now had two letters, added two more, and became the first four-year letterman.) Rod actually ran the team because Sam did not come out until after the basketball season. "Little Artie," as Rod always called me, became his second baseman. I had beefed up all the way to 125 pounds—my top playing weight.

In 1948, we won our first national championship in baseball. In the finals, we pulled a triple play in the last inning of the first game to win 3-1. We lost the first game of a doubleheader the next day, 8-3, but won the deciding game, 9-2. I went 6 for 11 with two or three walks in the series.

After graduation, I signed with the New York Yankees and played pro ball for six years before beginning a long coaching career. It all started with that phone call from Rod. He taught me how to play the game right. He built my confidence. Whatever success I've had, I owe to him. I've never known anyone else like him. I am grateful to God for putting him in my life.

Mickey McNamee
(Outfielder)

My junior year, we opened the collegiate schedule with a three game series versus Fresno State in Fresno. Single game Friday with a twilight doubleheader on Saturday. We traveled by bus to those games. Games are over late, and we head for home. About 2 a.m., the bus pulls into a truck stop south of Bakersfield. Virtually everyone on the bus was asleep but me. Therefore, I observed Rod exit the bus as a gentleman exited from the office. They called each by name, shook hands, hugged, and carried on a conversation like two lost friends reuniting. I couldn't believe what I was witnessing considering the environment. It was a lesson I observed over and over again for nearly 50 years. Outwardly, he treated everyone with respect and kindness. He made people feel special in his presence. A life lesson learned at 2 a.m. in the morning at a truck stop.

Coach made everyone that he kept on the team feel as if they were important to the success of the team. They were commonly referred to as the double XXers. Pitchers and catchers toiled especially hard for the benefit of the team. Their reward was an old uniform, a seat in the bullpen, and playing time as part of the infamous L.A. All-Stars. They didn't quit and seldom complained. It was a lesson for a soon-to-be career coach who patterned his game after the greatest college baseball coach of all time.

When coming to USC from a very strong junior college program that was the state baseball champions, it was an easy transition. Why? Because our coach (the author) was a former player and assistant coach for Rod. The similarities between the two programs were at times spooky. But for one player, it proved to be a significant advantage. USC and Coach Dedeaux attracted the best players from all over. Having a working knowledge of how his system worked and what his expectations were gave this player an opportunity he will always cherish. Success breeds success, and it all started with number one.

Russ McQueen
(Pitcher)

One should never have mistaken Rod's jaunty and relaxed demeanor for a lack of competitive drive. He wanted to win and expected to win most of the time. He also expected to win when something big was on the line or when our backs were against the wall. As competitive as he was on the field, however, he was a peacemaker everywhere else. Once, at a late night diner in Omaha, the two counter waitresses were fighting—name calling, cursing, even throwing things at each other. It was quite a show for the small handful of us in the cafe at the midnight hour. We watched the show and ducked when necessary. As we left the diner, I looked back to see Rod huddled with the two combatants, a hand on each shoulder, speaking to them about getting along and being a team. He was teaching, encouraging, and showing compassion. The ladies, nodding frequently, were listening respectfully and intently. Rod the peacemaker and teacher had their attention. Soon, the women were hugging each other and crying. It turned out they were sisters.

Rod's sense of humor was inspiring. When he was in his late 80s and using a walker (at least, he used it when Justin was watching), he made a trip down to Havana, Cuba, with the USC baseball team. I tagged along as well, bringing my father. It was great fun, with several games against Cuban provincial teams and a fair amount of great sightseeing. One evening, the entire entourage went out to dinner at a restaurant located in one of those picturesque but rundown Spanish style buildings in Old Havana. As rundown as it was on the outside, the inside was a disaster. The entrance into the lobby revealed what had once been an ornate, curved staircase with a once-beautiful balustrade leading to an upstairs landing. We waited for Rod to make his way up that staircase, with assistance from Justin. The banister wobbled as if in an earthquake, and pieces were coming off. Upon reaching the top, Rod looked back down toward us and scanned the large and once opulent but now devastated room below him. With perfect timing, he lifted his cane and his free arm and yelled "Power to the people."

June 1972: It was the final game of the College World Series. The night before, Randy Scarberry had pitched a complete game win over the Arizona State University Sun Devils, who previously had no losses to our one, earning us a final shot against them. In other words, we had to beat them twice in a row to win the championship.

On this final evening, senior right-hander Mark Sogge started and courageously held ASU scoreless into the bottom of the fifth inning, when Mark's sore arm caught up with him. The score was 1-0 in our favor, as we had scored a run on a passed ball against the great ASU right-hander Jim Crawford. You might expect a head coach to be a bit intense and tight in such circumstances, but if you anticipated that from Rod, you would be mistaken. He was always loose, confident, and seemed sure the Trojans would prevail. I was called in from the bullpen, having been warned by Rod earlier that he would summon me as early as midgame if necessary. I walked onto the mound with the bases loaded and no outs to find Rod smiling and tossing the ball casually up and down. His words: "Hello, Rusty. Situation normal—bases loaded, nobody out. Go get 'em." Then, he jauntily left the infield, as if it was no more than a practice game. Catcher Sam Ceci and I looked at each other for a second, shrugged, and said, "Let's go to work." Final score: USC 1, ASU 0.

Jerry Merz
(Pitcher)

As the bottom of the ninth began, USC was down 7-0 and Winfield had a one-hitter and 15 strikeouts. The first hitter was Ken Huizenga pinch hitting for pitcher Brian Hueblein. He hit a ball that just got through up the middle for a single. Next up was the leadoff man: Left-handed-hitting center fielder Creighton Tevlin (the only one to not strike out) hits a grounder to the second baseman. They get one out at second, and in a bang-bang play at first, Tevlin is called safe. At this point, with only two outs to record in the game and ahead 7-0, Minnesota's head coach, Dick Siebert (an 11-year veteran of MLB), runs out to protest the call and is ejected from the game. Are you kidding me?

Well, as we all know, "the rest is history." Here's the point: Maybe he was the smartest man in the house. Maybe he didn't think he had enough of a lead? The next out they recorded would be the eighth hitter after Tevlin: Ken Huizenga again, who hit a sacrifice fly to score Ed Putnam to tie the game at 7-7. Marvin Cobb entered to pinch run for Dennis Littlejohn at first and with Tevlin at bat took off to steal second. Unbelievably, the Minnesota catcher delivered a great throw to second, but Cobb was safe in a very close play. Tevlin delivers a single up the middle and Cobb scores. Game over.

Some of Coach's comments after the game included: "I think I saw Cobb touch dirt five times on his run from second to score standing up." "I still thought we were in the game." "They made a mistake and made the Trojan's mad." Note: In the top of the ninth, up 7-0, Minnesota attempted to drag bunt to get on and, when they got someone on, tried to bunt the runner to second and into scoring position. Siebert was right: They didn't have enough of a lead.

George Milke
(Pitcher)

Spring of 1972: I was being recruited by USC while in high school at Marian. A "die hard Trojan" by the name of Monroe "Bookie" Clark (friend of Rod's) brought me up to USC to throw against the Trojans just before heading out to Omaha. I threw for the Downey Reds—two innings. I guess I threw pretty well. Next thing I know, Bookie and I are up in Rod's office in Heritage Hall. Rod sits me and Bookie down (once Bookie got his crutches out of the way) and asked me if I wanted to be a Trojan. I was very excited to say the least and said yes immediately. ... Bookie [almost] started to cry. Bookie and my dad (Bud) were good friends, and my dad knew of Bookie's trials and tribulations (health problems) growing up. He graduated from USC in 1947 (Kappa Alpha Order [KAO] fraternity member) and was as "die-hard Trojan" as they come. I couldn't have been prouder for Bookie to be there in my dad's stead, as he could not make the trip up from Chula Vista.

This is highlighting Bookie more than Rod, but it lends to the type of person Rod was. Here you have this little man—withered by polio over the years—never complaining about his situation—and was such a dear friend of Rod's. Bookie epitomized that Trojan spirit. Much of that spirit was given to Bookie via Rod. Rod was able to look into the hearts of people—not just their frame, mph of their fastball, how quick they got down the line, or their prowess at swinging the Shillelagh. Bookie was at every game with Bud during that 1974 campaign in Omaha and was invited to the team dinner after we won it. He knew he had a part in that championship.

1974 trip to Omaha: We were on the plane back to our second home: Omaha. Halfway there, Justin comes back and talks to me a bit—how you feeling ... ready to go type of pep talk, which he did with everyone. Justin then says, "Come with me—number one wants to talk with you. Well, needless to say, I had no clue what about. We get up to first class (Rod always said "It only takes a dime more to go first class, tiger") and sits me down and says—I will never forget—"Georgie, we like what you have been doing on the mound recently and we want you to be the opening pitcher versus Texas. ... We think you are ready to go. You ready to go, tiger?" Ready to go—I calmly but confidently said: "Yes, Coach. I can't wait to take the mound versus Texas." ... The thing I remember to this day: Coach always mentioning "we." Not I want *you* to or I need *you* to or I expect this from *you*. ... It was always *we*. Something I took into my teaching and coaching career—now going on 28 years of. I think all of us realize what an impact—what an influence—Rod had on us. Not just the baseball ideology but life's lessons. How to be the best you can at whatever you do. Rod prepared us for life after baseball—very much as our fathers did.

1975 versus Arizona State at Dedeaux Field: We were down vs. ASU 3-1 in the top of the seventh. Garret Strong was at the plate, Kenny Landreaux on third, 2 and 0 count to Strong. Floyd Bannister on the hill for the Sun Devils keeping us in check—I was keeping us in the game—barely. Next pitch—boom—line drive right back at me, nails me in the left eye, and just went over my glove. … I thought I was dead. My teammates thought I was dead. People in the stands thought I was dead. I am trying to remain conscious—which I do—blood everywhere. They cart me off the field to Madeline's "Conquest"—my fingers raised in true Trojan fashion—they stitch me up in Heritage Hall (there's a USC doc in the stands). I am in the hospital for two days of observations. Rod comes in to visit. He says: "We are going to Tempe for the tournament tomorrow. We will be praying for you (I never did know at that time Rod was Catholic). When we return, we want you ready to go versus USF [the University of San Francisco] at Candlestick." … I was just hoping to see out of the eye once again. [But I was] on the mound versus USF—Rod got me back on that horse again as soon as possible. … Rod and the Big Trojan in the sky. (ASU won, and, yes, Landreaux scored.)

1998 USC baseball banquet: I was fortunate enough to be on the dais at the USC baseball banquet that was honoring Rod as the college baseball Coach of the Century in addition to recognizing another NCAA Champion for USC—the 1998 team coached by Mike Gillespie. It was a spectacular event. I was humbled when asked to speak along with some very distinguished Trojans—me being the lowest on that totem pole. I had the opportunity to speak about Rod and what he meant—as all of us did. All of the "Rodisms": one set of rules, tiger; only cost a dime more to go first class; Bussy, bussy— whack it to 'em. You're driving the champs; "McNamara's Band"; See's® chocolate in the dugout via Dusty; wearing the wig; Tiger, what time is it?; Shift those puppies, tiger—and many more. What I concluded with was in speaking of a dear friend—my roomy at USC: Pete Redfern. … Pete had a diving accident that ended his baseball career. He broke his neck and that was all she wrote. Pete lost his dad when he was 14 and his mom shortly after making his major league debut (he was with the Twins versus the Angels in Anaheim). Rod continued to embrace Pete with all the Trojan vim and vigor for many years after—even up until Rod's passing. … Rod had a special place in his heart for Pete. I know that Pete cherished Rod and Helen, and he loved them dearly. Pete continues to be an inspiration to me as he exemplifies that Trojan mystic— that Trojan attitude. Rod's message that hit home with Pete before and after his accident (and surely resonates within us all to this day): "Never say die, tiger—never say die."

Ken Guffey Miller
(First Baseman)

I can't remember the number of times Rod would tell us "It's an honor and a privilege to play for USC." At first, these words went over my head. I was recruited to play baseball, and when I touched my feet to the infield or outfield grass, I believe this to be my opportunity. In time, I knew it was USC, its buildings, classes, and professors that held my future.

"I have one set of rules: Do everything right." This is one of Rod's classic sayings and one he made clear on our first day of our college careers. Rod expected each of us to be an "A" student not in economic or political science but in baseball. He drilled us over and over on the basics and fundamentals of the game. If you do everything right, good things happen.

Everyone has heard of the field of dreams, but few have heard the story of the 1959 team—the team of broken dreams. Most of the players on the '59 team had played on the '58 national championship team and were poised to repeat. The team started the season ranked number one in the country and for good reason. All four starting pitchers were returning as well as most position players.

Shock and disbelief was felt by all when the NCAA sanctioned USC for football violations. Sanctions were assessed not only on football but on all sports programs, eliminating our chance to go for the national title. Demoralized, the team continued on with its number one ranking all through the season—now a team of broken dreams. When the season ended, the team had a school record batting average of .325 and an amazing school record of 9.7 runs per game.

The surprise shock happened at season's end. When final team rankings come out, it's customary that the team that wins the College World Series is ranked number one. This year, the coaches of America had USC sitting on top of the rankings above the College World Series winner [Oklahoma State University]. This had never happened before and has never happened since.

[The Los Angeles] Dodgers offered to fly the College World Series winner to Los Angeles all expenses paid for a two-game series with USC, but they [Oklahoma State] turned the offer down.

Years later, our coach would state on several occasions that the 1959 team was the best team he ever coached. With the spotlight at USC on the 12 baseball national championships, memories of the '59 team are all but forgotten. For the team of broken dreams, only the players remember the achievements of this great team and what might have been.

Bill Olson
(Outfielder)

One memory comes immediately to mind, which illustrates Coach Dedeaux's sense of humor: During the team's July–August 1955 tour of Japan, we were taking a train to our destination. On pulling into the station but before the train had come to a "full and complete stop," I stood and retrieved my bag from an overhead rack. The train lurched and the bag grazed (she might have said struck or slammed into) a lady's head. The lady turned out to be an American Army captain's wife who wasn't placated by my profuse apologies and wasn't in a forgiving mood.

Forward about 30 years: A few of us nostalgic types thought it would be nice to have a get-together of those who were on that trip. The first time we got together with Rod for a planning meeting, he greeted me with: "Hi, Billy. … We just received a letter from that lady you hit on the train in Japan, and she is suing for damages."

Another memory from that same tour: On our last day in Japan, we played (and beat) a Japanese university in Tokyo. After the game, many of us discarded our baseball undergarments in the locker room to make more room in our luggage for gifts we had purchased. After being hosted at a farewell dinner by the Far East Air Force (FEAF), we went to the airport. While we stood around waiting for our flight to be called, four well-dressed Japanese arrived and, bowing, presented us with our laundered underwear. With USC's face at stake, Coach immediately dispatched someone to purchase some flowers so we could reciprocate in real time. Can't remember how long this took, but I'm sure he charmed them with thanks and maybe a little double-talk.

It was great to play for a winner.

Randy Port
(Infielder/Outfielder)

I happily played and lettered for Rod in 1967, 1968 (NCAA champs), and 1969. Coach Dedeaux had a profound and wonderful impact on my life, and I have always experienced personal joy every time his teachings are shared with my family and many friends over these many years. I was offered a contract to sign with the Angels organization right out of Birmingham high school in Van Nuys in 1965 but opted to follow my dream instead to play for Rod at USC in the quest for championships while also gaining a business degree. I consider that decision to have been a blessing and well worth it for so many reasons, which I will enumerate.

My younger brother, Jeff, played for Rod in 1970, 1971, and 1972 (three straight NCAA titles), and Jeff became team captain in 1972. Jeff was named all-Pac-8 third baseman in 1971, was a starter when chosen on the Pan American team, and was drafted by the Dodgers—all during that same year—but Jeff passed on signing with the Dodgers to stay as part of a third in a row run at the time for another title. Unfortunately, after being injured his senior year, he couldn't carry on his career upon graduating or we all may have heard of Jeff Port, not Ron Cey, as the Dodger third baseman for those many celebrated years well into the 1980s. Also, Jeff's son, Ryan, my nephew, played on the 1998 NCAA championship team. So, our Port family is proudly part of five Trojan baseball championships.

After my introduction by Justin Dedeaux to Pat Haden at our last baseball alumni dinner at Galen, I asked Pat if that was "special trivia" for our family in Trojan folklore to have been part of five titles. He cutely answered promptly that Rob Adolph *himself* was part of six NCAA titles: four baseball and two football in the early 1970s. So, we just laughed about his bursting my bubble of a special slice of Trojan history for our family, for which my Dad would have been so proud. Also, for the record, when my dad, Al Port, longtime Trojan booster, passed in 1993, our family donated in his memory the first electric scoreboard at Dedeaux Field, along with a Hall of Fame facility to help share all the Trojan baseball great's folklore. Some of my favorite Deadeauxisms are:

- "When the going gets tough, the Trojans get going and the Bruins go shopping." This one is a classic and always makes me laugh or lighten up during difficult times. I have had several heart surgeries that have, thank God, been successful. But I never fail to think of this saying before entering each one to help me get through it all. I have to admit, thoughts of family certainly come first, but good, positive Trojan memories greatly enhance that.

- "On any fly, the fielder repeatedly yells out 'I have it.'—not 'I got it.'" (You're in college now—learn proper English, right?) Got a kick out of sharing and teaching these sayings while coaching my daughter's softball team years ago.

- "Don't think—you're hurting the team." In 1967, while I was coaching first base during one crucial game, I yelled out and motioned to our batter trying to stretch a single into a double to hold at first, but he ran through my verbal shouts and hand signals to be thrown out, as the saying goes, "from me to you." Coach immediately motions and yells out "Hey, tiger, come over here" and while in the dugout with him asked what was he trying to do. The player started to answer with "Sorry, Coach, I was just thinking." At that moment, Coach interrupted and softly answered back, "Tiger, don't think—you're hurting the team. We don't make mental mistakes. We tried to hold you up, but by you thinking it was better to run through his sign, you embarrassed the team and, more importantly, [ruined] our chances to win." In fairness, this was a young starter who did learn from it thereafter. What was most impressive to me was the coach's class, style, and low-key manner in handling this.

- My favorite five-star Dedeauxism was when one of our Trojan rookies while at bat popped up and instead of running full speed with his head, he threw his bat in disgust and only trotted toward first. So, coach motions for him as he was returning to the dugout to come see him, at which time Coach, in a soft, almost quizzical tone, says, "Tiger," as they are standing almost nose to nose, "you always run out at full speed on any pop-up." Then, with a straight face and most of our team within earshot, Coach looks him right in the eye and says "How do you know that that might have been the first pop-up that never came down and you could have been standing at second base?" Needless to say, the rest of the team all rolled their eyes laughing after hearing that one.

Last to share is that in 1968, when we were the NCAA champs, no one would even believe either in a movie or script that we ever should have made it to Omaha. In a best two out of three playoff to qualify for that year's College World Series, we faced Cal State at Los Angeles. Here's the ridiculous, totally crazy part: In the deciding third game after splitting the first two, we are the visiting team, and going to the top of the ninth, we are down 4-1 with two outs and nobody on. Only because of Coach's instilled belief in us as winning Trojans did we still believe we could come back, and incredibly— and almost unbelievably—we did. It felt like a complete out of body experience that we all were witnessing this miracle. After that, we predictably became the team of destiny and even in each game in Omaha. We were down in every game but one going into the seventh inning or beyond. Yet, we believed with no doubt that we would come back by pulling for each other with every single teammate standing up and yelling encouragement in support of each to our players at bat. To me, it's almost inexplicable and yet will always give us the invincible feeling that no matter what you face in life going forward, don't ever, ever give up. So, it wasn't just a saying that "When the going gets tough, the Trojans get going." It became a core belief for the rest of our lives in whatever we may do.

Buddy Pritchard
(Second Baseman)

I was never knowingly recruited by Rod. During the city playoffs, while I was hitting in one of those enclosed city cage/backstops, I overheard Rod say, "But can he hit a curveball?" The next pitch was a big roundhouse curveball that I hit for a home run. He approached me after the game and asked me to write him a note expressing my interest in attending USC. I complied with his request, and to this day, I'm embarrassed that I addressed the letter to "Coach Rod Dado."

Prior to my junior year, Rod gave me a haircut and a shave, explaining to me that if I would move from shortstop to second base, the versatility could help my professional career. (He really wanted Billy Faddis to play shortstop). As it turned out, he was right because I stuck around for nine years in pro ball.

During the winter prior to my senior year, the Pittsburgh Pirates offered me a sizable bonus. I went to Rod and told him if he wanted me to stay, I wouldn't leave. He advised me to sign. I'm sure he felt I would never be offered this type bonus again, but he could also use it against the NCAA. They had ruled that because of a football rules infraction that baseball as well as other sports would not be eligible for post-season competition. So, Rod claimed that I had signed as result of the injustice perpetrated on the baseball program by the NCAA.

Phil Alden Robinson*
(Director, *Field of Dreams*)

All of the ballplayers in the movie were prepped for the film by Rod Dedeaux. He coached at USC for many years and is a wonderful man—very full of life, energetic, very supportive, just really was very giving of himself and cheerful all the time, was a great spirit to have around. And one day, we were in between setups, and I said, "Hey, Coach, what position did you play?" He said, "I was a shortstop." I said, 'Really? Could you— were you good?' He got very quiet and he said, "I could field the ball." I said, "Could

*Source: Director's commentary recorded for the anniversary edition DVD of *Field of Dreams*

you hit?" He said, "I could hit the ball." And he was strangely quiet. And I said to him, "Well, how come you never played in the majors?" And he said, "I did." I said, "Really?" [Dedeaux said,] "Yes, in 1930-something." I forget what year he said. He was the starting shortstop for the Brooklyn Dodgers. He played one game, broke his back, and that was the end of his career. And I just blanched.

I said, "My God, you're Doc Graham." He said, "That's right." And I said, "Do you ever think about, 'Gee, the career I might've had.'" And he said, "Every day." He said it very quietly. It was very out of character for him, and I was so touched by that. And I did look him up in the Baseball Encyclopedia: He did go, I think, 1-for-4 with an RBI. That was his lifetime stats. So, having him be the man who trained all these fellows, including the kid who plays Doc Graham, was very meaningful to me, and I know it was to him too. It was great to have him around. I think about that often—about what that must have been like: to be good enough to start with a Major League team and, for one unlucky moment, not be able to do—the rest of your life takes another turn. What he did with that is, he put all of that emotion—which could have gone into bitterness or regret—into being a phenomenal coach. He sent more people to the majors than, I think, anybody else in college history. He's an amazing man.

Bob Santich
(Catcher)

One incident I remember most vividly was at Bovard Field. USC was playing Santa Clara, and I was sitting in my usual spot in the bullpen with the pitchers. Santa Clara had a man on first base when a double-play ball was hit and the runner goes way out of the base path to take out our shortstop, Freddy Scott. There is a huge collision and people are rolling in the dirt and a big fight starts. Jim Conroy, a blocking back on the USC football team, was sitting next to me, and he was the first one out on the field and in the middle of everything. He was punching and slugging, keeping three Santa Clara players busy at one time and loving every minute of it.

The president of the university was in the stands, and Coach Dedeaux ran out on the field attempting to break up the fight. You could hear him yelling: "C'mon, you guys. We are Trojans. Act like Trojans. You are representing your university. Get back into the dugout." It took most of our team to pry Conroy away from the fight and get him to the dugout. Coach Dedeaux had a scowl on his face as he ushered everyone back into the dugout. With that raspy voice you could hear for 400 feet, he made sure everyone knew our conduct was unbecoming of a Trojan athlete and was not the way he taught us to play. As he walked in the dugout, after everything was settled down, he looked right at Jim Conroy and said, "Atta way to hustle, tiger"—and 40 years later, "nothin's" changed.

Coach, thanks for giving me an opportunity to play for the greatest coach in collegiate baseball history and to be a part of USC's greatest team. Most of all, thanks for the opportunity to be a part of your DART team for these past 40 years. Congratulations for being named Coach of the Century. Atta way to hustle, tiger.

Jim Semon
(Pitcher)

In 1961, just before the Cal series, Rod had us in the locker room and made a speech that I will never forget. He went over the Cal roster scouting report and gave us the facts about each player, then said, "I wouldn't trade any one of you guys for any one of them." I felt he was looking at me personally, as did my teammates. We went out and won the series handily. I never got into any of the ball games, but I felt I was personally ready if called upon. The team was so jacked up, there was no stopping us. I personally carried those feelings into my coaching career and used that motivation technique to launch a successful baseball program at Chaffey High School. I am forever grateful to Rod for allowing me to be a part of that team, teaching me and later recommending me as a varsity baseball coach at Chaffey High School fresh out of USC.

Brent Strom
(Pitcher)

I remember:

- 1968, College World Series, Trojans versus Oklahoma State: Losing early second inning, bases loaded, 2-0 count brings me into the game, and Rod's only comment was: "Tiger, Tiger … Throw the ball down the middle and hope someone makes a play for you." I got an out on a pop-up and we went on to win the game and the series.
- 1970, senior season: Up in Seattle, we're winning 9-0. It's the bottom of the ninth with two outs, and I walk a guy on a 3-2 close pitch. Rod ended up fining me for doing so.
- 1970, Stanford: They beat us, fans rush the mound, there's a celebration. It's a Pac-8 game in the middle of the season, and Rod says this "tells us who we are, not them."

Steve Tanner
(Infielder)

Well, as it turns out, one game, the Fox decided to put me in the lineup and coach first base himself to show us how it was supposed to be done. We were at Bovard Field, and he was right in front of our dugout. As fate would have it, Oscar [Brown] got on first in the bottom of the first inning and (not surprisingly) promptly got picked off as Coach desperately yelled for him to "Get back." Having been fined for the same base coaching offense myself, I decided it would be a brilliant idea to fine Coach, so I wrote him down for $1 before the inning was over "for not getting Oscar back." Fortunately, I went out to shortstop when the next inning started, but all of my teammates who weren't in the lineup moved all the way down to the far end of the dugout to get out of harm's way. We were all laughing so hard, no one could even see straight. If I recall correctly, Coach Eddie Allen (another great guy) saw me doing it and looked the other way. It was all in good fun and not at all intended to be disrespectful, and Coach had the wisdom to know that.

From shortstop, I was looking right into the dugout, and I watched the Fox walk to the fine pad to write Oscar up for getting picked off. He paused ever so slightly, and with barely any perceptible reaction, just wrote up Oscar and sat down very calmly in his corner of the dugout nearest home plate without letting on at all, but I swear I saw the slyest, wryest smile on his face. The entire rest of the team was at the other end of the dugout doing their best to control themselves. Coach never spoke of the "incident" until years later at an alumni game when we were chatting about life and times, and I asked him if he remembered getting fined for getting Oscar picked off, and he smiled the really big smile of his and said he knew it was me all along and that he loved it, and we laughed really hard. He said he wasn't going to give me the satisfaction of acknowledging it and that he was doing everything he could not to laugh out loud.

Coach always called me "young Billy," since my Dad was named Bill, except when he was telling me to "Move my puppies," in which case, he called me "Tiger," like everyone else who was screwing up the fundamentals. Coach and I had our differences about the level of my talent, but we were always friends, and I admired him greatly—and still do to this day. His sense of humor and warmth were very endearing, and his reaction to my mischief was just one example of his fun-loving nature. Perhaps that is why I was the only player to have to wear the wig twice my sophomore year, but it was worth it.

Dave Van Gorder
(Catcher)

As things were winding down in the locker room after we had just defeated Arizona State University 10-3 in the 1978 national championship, a few of us older players were standing with coach as he reached into the cooler and pulled out a cold Budweiser. As he popped the top, he said, "The beer is always colder when you are a champion." As we got on the bus to head to our championship party, Coach said to the bus driver, "Whack it to 'em, bussy—you are really driving the champs."

Conclusion

Quite by accident, over the years, I've crossed paths with people who had come in contact with Rod briefly, also by accident. "You played for Rod Dedeaux. I said hello to him once at Dodger Stadium. He stopped and we exchanged a few words. I don't remember what was said. But he took a minute with a total stranger."

I heard words to that effect from, say, half a dozen people. All gave the same report. Rod made pleasant exchanges with strangers seem like the most natural thing in the world. One USC alumnus said that at a banquet, Rod even stepped away from a small group to return the man's greeting. He didn't just nod. He didn't just wave. He didn't act as though he was conferring grace. "He acted almost as if he knew me." I said, "Did he call you 'tiger'?" He said, "No." I said, "You hadn't made the club yet."

This book relies on Rod's players, friends, associates, and family for information. But beyond this circle, Rod must have met hundreds of people. He was not a greeter or a glad-hander. He never went out of his way to make his presence known. (Save when he was hamming it up.) When people recognized him, he recognized them. If only for a moment, they counted. I like to think they remembered him not because he was famous but because of how he behaved.

Epilogue

"My tastes are simple. All I demand is perfection."

Rod Dedeaux would always say that with a laugh and a twinkle in his eye. But deep down, he really meant it. He drove himself to achieve excellence in everything he touched. From his early years as a student and athlete, he was always at the head of the class. In his business life, he built a successful company and real estate empire with his fierce determination and attention to detail. "The Devil is in the details," he would so often say.

His coaching record and contributions to the game he loved are without parallel. I was privileged to play for him and then experience, as an assistant coach, a championship run that will never be equaled. While no man should be judged by wins or championships, it was a culmination of all his gifts and remarkable personality that allowed the Trojan baseball dynasty to set its place in baseball history.

He roared through life with a gusto and enthusiasm unmatched by anyone I have ever seen. I can speak for his family, business associates, fellow coaches, and his five decades of beloved players in saying that he was truly one of a kind—a true Trojan. Fight on!

Justin Dedeaux
Second Baseman

About the Author

David Rankin is a retired professor of English who holds a B.A. and M.A. from the University of Southern California and a Ph.D. from the University of London. He's widely published in his field and has won awards for teaching and for scholarship. He also worked closely with Educational Testing Service and the American Association of Medical Colleges to prepare placement and admissions tests.

Rankin was a pitcher at USC from 1951 to 1953, coached the freshman team for two seasons, and assisted Coach Dedeaux for two seasons. He coached the Coalinga Community College team that won the California State Championship in 1958.